The Heart

Other von Hildebrand books from St. Augustine's Press

The Nature of Love
The Dietrich von Hildebrand LiveGuide

The Heart

An Analysis of Human and Divine Affectivity

Dietrich von Hildebrand

Edited by John Henry Crosby

Preface by John Haldane
"Presentation" by John F. Crosby

ST. AUGUSTINE'S PRESS
South Bend, Indiana

in association with the Dietrich von Hildebrand Legacy Project
www.hildebrandlegacy.org

Manufactured in the United States of America.

2 3 4 5   23 22 21 20 19 18 17 16

Library of Congress Cataloging in Publication Data
Von Hildebrand, Dietrich, 1889-
    The heart : an analysis of human and divine affectivity /
    Dietrich von Hildebrand ; edited by John Henry Crosby ;
    preface by John Haldane; presentation by John F. Crosby. –
    [New ed.].
      p. cm.
    Includes index.
    ISBN 1-58731-357-X (hardbound: alk. paper)
    1. Sacred Heart, Devotion to. I. Crosby, John Henry.
    II. Title.
    BX2157.V6 2007
    233'.5 – dc22   2006034943

Paperbound edition ISBN: 978-1-58731-358-5

∞ The paper used in this publication meets the minimum requirements of the American National Standard for Information Sciences – Permanence of Paper for Printed Materials, ANSI Z39.48-1984.

ST. AUGUSTINE'S PRESS
www.staugustine.net

Et in medio nostri sit Christus Deus
dilectissimis in corde Jesu
Edithae et Eduardo

Contents

Why I Founded the Dietrich von Hildebrand Legacy Project

By John Henry Crosby

The Legacy Project had its inception in my desire to spend the year 2004 translating into English an assortment of German writings by Dietrich von Hildebrand. No sooner had I begun, however, than I realized that I was being presented with a *kairos*—a moment of opportunity that I might never have again. I saw the possibility of undertaking other translations, and even of undertaking other initiatives on behalf of the legacy of von Hildebrand. Alice von Hildebrand, the widow of Dietrich von Hildebrand, saw these opportunities with me and has wholeheartedly supported the work of the Legacy Project from the very beginning.

The mission of the Legacy Project is to engage the contemporary world, both Christian and secular, by uncovering and disseminating the buried treasure of Dietrich von Hildebrand's thought and witness. We plan to accomplish this in the following ways:

1. By translating into English the many writings of von Hildebrand from their original German and seeing to their publication;

2. By bringing important English writings of von Hildebrand back into print;

3. By giving special attention to distributing and disseminating our publications;

4. By collecting systematically the remembrances of von Hildebrand by those who had known him;

5. By establishing and developing a von Hildebrand website (www.hildebrandlegacy.org), to disseminate knowledge about von Hildebrand, to bring together those interested in his thought, and to offer a wide variety of resources to those studying von Hildebrand;

6. By publishing a quarterly newsletter, called *Transformation*;

7. By cataloguing and electronically preserving the unpublished papers, notes, and correspondence of von Hildebrand;

8. By sponsoring lectures, conferences, and other public events that will bring attention to the thought of von Hildebrand and set it in relation to the various streams of contemporary thought.

I am often asked why I founded the Legacy Project. How is it that a young man of 25 should devote himself to the work of appropriating, preserving, and disseminating the legacy of von Hildebrand? The answer begins in the close bond of friendship that connected my family to von Hildebrand many years before I was born. It is hard to imagine my maternal grandfather and my parents without the profound and formative relation they had to von Hildebrand. And while I never knew von Hildebrand personally (he died in 1977, the year before I was born), throughout my teenage years I had the privilege of coming to know Alice von Hildebrand. My appreciation for von Hildebrand grew especially during my university years. I felt increasingly that his rich and abundant vision of the world was becoming my own, and I began to understand why generations had been nourished by his prolific writings. Above all, I saw how true were the words which Cardinal Joseph Ratzinger had written about von Hildebrand in the year 2000, and I quote:

> I am personally convinced that, when, at some time in the future, the intellectual history of the Catholic Church in the twentieth century is written, the name of Dietrich von Hildebrand will be most prominent among the figures of our time.

Dietrich von Hildebrand was a philosopher I could *follow*. His heroic struggle against Nazism fired my imagination; his single-minded love and pursuit of truth presented me with a vivid embodiment of the true philosopher; and his passion for music, literature, and art taught me that life without beauty is impoverished and inhuman.

The Legacy Project is my response to the gift that Dietrich von Hildebrand has been in my life, and I am deeply aware that I am acting on behalf of the thousands who received this same gift in their own lives.

As the founder of the Legacy Project, I must acknowledge the special inspiration and support of two Popes—John Paul II and Benedict XVI. To John Paul II, I owe the sense of vocation that emerged from his many "calls"—to the youth, to evangelists, and, of special importance for me, to *philosophers* who were inspired by their Philosopher-Pope to explore the natural mysteries of the world, to use the common language of philosophy to engage secular thinkers in dialogue, to draw on the resources of both traditional and contemporary philosophy, and to defend truth with courage and conviction. From the very start of his pontificate, John Paul had been calling for the renewal and regeneration of philosophy. I saw in the writings of von Hildebrand a remarkable anticipation of this call and the opportunity to offer a unique and timely response. Though John Paul died soon after the founding of the Legacy Project, he still knew of its existence and conveyed his apostolic blessing.

Likewise, Pope Benedict has played a central role in the work of the Legacy Project. His loyalty to John Paul, his deeply intelligent defense of the faith, and his own philosophical and theological contributions have inspired and motivated the Legacy Project. And not only is Pope Benedict a great admirer of von Hildebrand, prior to his elevation to the papacy he even joined the Legacy Project as an Honorary Member. As Pope, his continuing support has been concrete and vital. It is with joy that we join him as "laborers in the vineyard of the Lord."

Three indispensable friends deserve the special distinction of "co-founder." Alice von Hildebrand, wife and faithful messenger of her husband's thought and witness, has supported the Legacy Project from the first day of its existence. Without her there would be no Legacy Project. Then there is my father, John F. Crosby, himself a student and disciple of von Hildebrand, from whom I received my philosophical *eros* and my undying passion for all things von Hildebrandian. He is my collaborator and patient advisor in every aspect of the Legacy Project. Last but not least, I must mention my great and dear friend, Anthony Gualandri, who has served the Legacy Project as Director of Special Projects for nearly two years. There is no question that without Anthony's patient, intelligent, and deeply committed efforts, the Legacy Project would be a shadow of what it is today.

And so, on this occasion of the first publication of the Legacy Project, it is my honor and joy to thank the many friends whose support, financial and otherwise, helped to bring the Legacy Project into existence:

Advisory Council of the Legacy Project, Butch and Pat Bercier, Robin M. Bobak, Hedy K. Boelte, Christopher Briggs, Archbishop Raymond Leo Burke, Ronda Chervin, James V. Coffey, George C. Creel, Anne Crosby, John and Pia Crosby, Josef Crosby, Chris and Carol Cuddeback, Kevin and Kateryna Cuddeback, Michael and Suzanne Doherty, Stanislaw Cardinal Dziwisz, Greg Erlandson, Alexander Fedoryka, Damian & Irene Fedoryka, Daniel Fedoryka, Maria Fedoryka, Jeffrey M. Fehn, Bruce Fingerhut, Fr. Hermann Geißler, Robert P. George, Michael and Mary Georgopulos, Lynne Gerken, Bernard B. Gilligan, Augusta O. Gooch, Edward and Alice Ann Grayson, Ingrid A. Gregg, Carrie R. Gress, Anthony C. Gualandri, John M. Haas, John Haldane, Gerard and Karen Hanley, Nicholas J. Healy, Jr., Paul and Barbara Henkels, Michelle Hogan, James M. Hostetler, Thomas Howard, Robert D. Hurt, Magdalena Hutton, Michael C. Jordan, Paulette L. Kardos, Andreas A. M. Kinneging, Annette Y. Kirk, Edward J. Kondracki, Robert L. Kreppel, Bishop Andreas Laun, John and Madeline LeBlanc, Ryan K. Lovett, Frank and Patricia Lynch, Donald W. Maliniak, Donald and Margaret Maroldy, Lee and Margaret Matherne, William E. May, Judith Fife Mead, Michael J. Miller, Gerard and Germana Mitchell, Lynn Moseley, Suzanne C. Murphy, Thomas J. Nash, Eileen M. Nielsen, Michael Novak, Kevin and Dawn O'Scannlain, Edmund D. Pellegrino, Leon J. Podles, Dana P. Robinson, Ronald J. Rychlak, Rex and Barbara Sanders, William L. Saunders, Jr., Fr. Paul Scalia, Stephen D. Schwarz, Josef and Mary Seifert, Barry Smith, Mark T. Smith, Robert and Joan Smith, Madeleine F. Stebbins, Enzo Tatasciore, Jonathan D. Teichert, Frederick Teichert, Jules and Kathleen van Schaijik, Scott Walter, Fritz K. Wenisch, and Gregory C. Woodward.

Last but not least, I must thank several foundations whose munificent support has been decisive in the establishment of the Legacy Project—the Earhart Foundation, the Our Sunday Visitor Institute, the Papal Foundation, the Raskob Foundation for Catholic Activities, the R. Templeton Smith Foundation, and the Charles A. Mastronardi Foundation.

Preface

By John Haldane

For many years the subject of the emotions, and more that of the affective side of human nature generally, was either neglected by philosophers or treated cursorily within the framework of an empiricist moral psychology that consigned feelings to the sphere of subjective desire. It was not always so. Certainly passion was generally opposed to reason in the thought of antiquity, but in Thomas Aquinas there is a degree of recognition, based on Aristotle and scripture, of the normativity of emotional responses: feelings may be appropriate or inappropriate, well or badly grounded, and express virtuous or vicious dispositions.

The key to recovering this objectivist understanding for modern times was the rediscovery, first by the scholastically trained Franz Brentano, of the classical notion of intentionality or mental directedness. Just as beliefs are about "propositions" or states of affairs, and thoughts are of "things," so feelings have contents and "objects": I am happy *that* such and such is so; angry *about* this, fearful *of* that. The intentionality of emotion, developed in different ways in the philosophies of Edmund Husserl and Ludwig Wittgenstein, was a common theme of two books published in the early 1960s: Anthony Kenny's *Action, Emotion and Will* (1963) and Dietrich von Hildebrand's *The Heart* (1965). Though different in style and purpose, and though genuinely creative in their own ways, each work contains echoes of scholastic philosophical ideas: Kenny like Brentano had been a priest, educated in the thought of Aquinas, and von Hildebrand was a convert to the Catholic faith these others had left behind.

If *Action, Emotion and Will* is rigorous in pursuing logical detail, as befits a monograph intended for a professional academic readership, *The Heart* is the more expansive work, building upon the intentionality of emotion an account of the importance of this aspect of the human psyche, and making an effective case for the "heart" as the spiritual core of the person. It is worth stating in brief, and illustrating by quotation, some of von Hildebrand's central philosophical claims.

First, affectivity has generally been misinterpreted on account of failing to attend to the analogical nature of the term "feelings":

> The entire affective area, and even the heart, has been seen in the light of bodily feelings, emotional states, or passions in the strict sense of the term. And what is rightly denied to these types of "feelings," is unjustly and erroneously denied to affective experiences such as value-responding joy, a deep love, a noble enthusiasm. . . . (the term "feeling" is thus anything but univocal) (pp. 4–5).

It is interesting to note in passing the parallel with Kenny's discussion of "feelings" in his chapter of the same name (Ch. 3):

> There are genuine analogies between feelings of emotion and the objects of the senses. . . . Duration, intensity, and blending are properties shared by feelings of all kinds, whether perceptions, sensations or emotions. . . . But the dissimilarities between emotions and perceptions are more significant than the similarities (pp. 56–7).

Second, for von Hildebrand, an emotional response can only properly be understood and evaluated in connection with its object:

> As soon as the affective response is deprived of the object which has engendered it and from which its meaning and justification stem . . . the affective response is reduced to a mere affective state (p. 6).

Compare again, a parallel from Kenny's book:

> The most important difference between a sensation and an emotion is that emotions, unlike sensations are essentially directed to objects. . . .
>
> The language of the emotions must therefore be taught not only in connection with emotional behaviour, but above all in connection with the objects of emotion (pp. 60 & 66).

Third, the "heart" is distinct from the "intellect" and the "will":

Augustine's Press, for his meticulous work on the layout of the text; to John Haldane, for writing the preface; and to Katharina M. Seifert who, along with Anthony C. Gualandri, designed the cover.

The editor wishes to acknowledge Rudolf Bernet, director of the Husserl Archive in Louvain, for granting permission to publish a translation of Edmund Husserl's evaluation of von Hildebrand's dissertation, as well as Ignatius Press for granting permission to quote Joseph Cardinal Ratzinger's words about von Hildebrand on the dust jacket of this volume.

John Henry Crosby
Founder & Director
Dietrich von Hildebrand Legacy Project
November 2006

Editorial Note

It is with great pride that the Dietrich von Hildebrand Legacy Project presents this new edition of *The Heart*. Out of print for over thirty years, this volume not only represents the return into circulation of an important work by a major Catholic philosopher and theologian, it is also the first fruit of the Legacy Project's efforts to preserve and promote the intellectual and spiritual riches of Dietrich von Hildebrand.

Originally written in English, the first edition of *The Heart* was published by Helicon Press in 1965 under the title, *The Sacred Heart*. A 1977 reprint by Franciscan Herald Press shortened the title to *The Heart*. The present edition of *The Heart* contains the complete text of the 1965/1977 edition, the only difference being that von Hildebrand's original introduction has, with the consent of Alice von Hildebrand, been moved to the end of the book as an afterword. Given the philosophical focus of the first part and the religious focus of the second and third parts of *The Heart*, it was thought that the introduction, itself religious in nature, would better be read in connection with these latter sections.

For this new edition, the entire text of *The Heart* was carefully reviewed and very lightly edited. Because English was not von Hildebrand's native language, the text of *The Heart* frequently exhibits the influence of German grammar and of Germanic expressions. The editor attempted to "anglicize" the text, making the English as natural as possible. In addition, the editor corrected any mistakes of punctuation and spelling.

The preparation of this volume has been the labor of many hands. Special thanks are due to John F. Crosby, for contributing an introduction and for participating in every aspect of the editorial process; to Kathleen van Schaijik, who meticulously reviewed the entire text; to Bruce Fingerhut of St. Augustine's Press, for his patience in working with the fledgling Legacy Project; to Benjamin Fingerhut, also of St.

to certain younger philosophers closely associated with me (Scheler, Pfänder, Reinach), he never falls into patterns of slavish discipleship. He goes his own way as an independent thinker and often enough opens new perspectives; as a result he even deepens our understanding of certain significant historical connections of ideas, concerning Kant for instance. The dissertation deals with the basic problems of systematically distinguishing among the various ethical value qualities and among the bearers of these qualities. For the most part, previous ethical thought did not do justice to the great variety of bearers in which value predicates immediately inhere; it was deficient in the necessary phenomenological analysis of what is primordial in this area. The author attempts to fill this gap, to bring to evidence all the relevant phenomenological levels, and to analyze them with clarity. In his aspiration to reach ultimate foundations he goes far beyond the sphere of ethical phenomena and ventures with some success into the deepest problems of a general phenomenology of consciousness. But the real strength of this work and its most significant and original results concerning the affective sphere are mainly to be found in the analyses that fill Part II, chapters 3–8. We are simply astonished at the incomparably intimate knowledge that the author has of the various formations of affective consciousness and of the objective correlates of affective consciousness.

Having said all of this I can only propose for this important dissertation the distinction *opus eximium*.[4]

---

4 The highest distinction that could be awarded to a dissertation.

was formed in the school of Husserl and was, as Husserl says, deeply indebted to Max Scheler, Alexander Pfänder, and Adolf Reinach. Now one of the great ideals of phenomenology is to avoid reductionism of all kinds, to let each thing be itself and not to run one thing into another. Only by practicing this phenomenological anti-reductionism is von Hildebrand able to achieve in this book the rehabilitation of affectivity that he intends. He thinks that the affective sphere has been wrongly reduced to other things in the human person, such as body feelings, or the will, and that only the resolute anti-reductionism of the phenomenologist can bring to evidence the logos and the genius of affectivity.

And our third reason for publishing Husserl's evaluation is that he touches at the end of it on *das Gemütsbewusstsein*, or affective consciousness, and reserves his highest praise for von Hildebrand's exploration of affective acts and their intentional correlates. Thus already in his first major work von Hildebrand distinguished himself as a philosopher of the heart. The present volume is a later (1965), philosophically fully mature development of what was first broached in the dissertation (1912). Even this earliest von Hildebrandian discussion of affectivity was judged by Husserl to be "astonishing."

Here is the text of Husserl's evaluation of von Hildebrand's dissertation, dated July 30, 1912[2]:

> I have read this dissertation with great delight. I would almost say that the genius of Adolf von Hildebrand[3] has been inherited by his son, the author, in the form of a philosophical genius. In fact in this work the author gives evidence of a rare talent to draw from the deep sources of phenomenological intuition, to analyze with intelligence and precision what he has seen, and to express it conceptually in a most rigorous way. Phenomenological research is here placed entirely in the service of major philosophical issues, for the solution of which it really prepares the way. Although the author is indebted for his understanding of phenomenological method and issues, as well as for particular points that he makes in various passages, to my lectures and writings, and although he is also indebted

2   The German text was found in the Husserl archive by Karl Schumann and was first published in *Aletheia* V (1992), 4–5.

3   Adolf von Hildebrand (1847–1921) was the father of Dietrich von Hildebrand and an eminent German sculptor of the late 19th and early 20th century.

Edmund Husserl's Evaluation of Dietrich von Hildebrand's Doctoral Dissertation

Presented and translated by John F. Crosby

The reader might be puzzled at the decision to publish in the present volume Edmund Husserl's evaluation of Dietrich von Hildebrand's doctoral dissertation, *Die Idee der sittlichen Handlung (The Concept of Moral Action)*. It might seem that the natural occasion for translating this evaluation would be the presentation of an English translation of the dissertation. And yet we have translated it for the present reissue of von Hildebrand's book, *The Heart*.

This we have done for three reasons. First, this evaluation is a remarkable testimony to von Hildebrand's significance as philosopher. To those who think that von Hildebrand was primarily a religious thinker but not really a philosopher, we say that the great master of phenomenology, under whom von Hildebrand wrote his dissertation in 1912, thought that von Hildebrand, already at the age of 22, was a gifted and original philosopher. As a matter of fact, Husserl's esteem for von Hildebrand's dissertation was even greater than indicated here in the evaluation. We now know through the important monograph of Karl Schumann on the Husserl-von Hildebrand relation that for years Husserl used von Hildebrand's dissertation in his own research into the foundations of ethics.[1] Such an acknowledgement of von Hildebrand by a thinker of Husserl's stature should catch the attention of people who are new to von Hildebrand as philosopher; it should gain from them a hearing for von Hildebrand, until they can see for themselves what kind of philosopher he is.

Our second reason for publishing in English Husserl's evaluation is that it underlines von Hildebrand's phenomenological origins. He

---

1 Karl Schumann, "Husserl und Hildebrand," in *Aletheia* V (1992), 6–33.

In this context "heart" means the focal point of the affective sphere, that which is most crucially affected with respect to all else in that sphere . . . the heart in this typical sense has the connotation of being the very center of gravity of all affectivity (p. 49).

Other important points follow in von Hildebrand's analysis: such as that happiness must be *felt* in order to be properly realised; that affective responses are objective when corresponding to the value of their objects; and that the heart is the spiritual center of the human psyche. I would recommend for special attention, however, what he has to say about the distinction between "tender" and "energized" affectivity (Ch. 3). Noting the liability of the former to lapse towards sentimentality he nonetheless emphasises its importance in relation to love (in its various categories) and defends it against those whose real target is what he terms "high values" and "true consciousness." Here von Hildebrand identifies not just a perennial possibility but a real, and currently pressing threat to true humanism; and as he notes with great insight, what announces itself as committed to fact and objectivity is in reality a form of closed subjectivism.

Von Hildebrand's book is a classic, a genuinely philosophical treatment offering insight yet with something of the accessibility of the writings of C.S. Lewis. It merits study by academic philosophers but also deserves to be as widely known and read among an educated public as are the works of that contemporary fellow searcher after the "permanent things." With the publication of this edition of *The Heart* those already familiar with von Hildebrand's writings have reason to celebrate, while new readers have the opportunity to enter into an exploration of issues that are at once eternal and immediate.

John Haldane
St. Andrews, Scotland
Easter Sunday, 2006

Part I
THE HUMAN HEART

CHAPTER ONE
The Role of the Heart*

The affective sphere, and the heart as its center, have been more or less under a cloud throughout the entire course of the history of philosophy. It has had a role in poetry, in literature, in the private prayers of great souls, and above all in the Old Testament, in the Gospel, and in the Liturgy, but not in the area of philosophy proper. In philosophy it has been treated like the proverbial stepson. This stepson-status not only refers to the fact that no place has been allotted to the exploration of the heart, but it also applies to the interpretation given the heart whenever it was dealt with.

The affective sphere, and with it the heart, has been excluded from the spiritual realm. It is true that we find in Plato's *Phaedrus* the words, "The madness of love is the greatest of heaven's blessings." But when it comes to a systematic classification of man's capacities (as in the *Republic*), Plato did not grant to the heart a rank comparable to that of the intellect.

But it is above all the role assigned to the affective sphere and to the heart in Aristotle's philosophy that evidences the ban placed on the heart. It must be said, however, that Aristotle did not consistently cling to this negative position concerning the affective sphere. For example, we find in the *Nicomachean Ethics* that "the good man not only wills the

---

* Throughout this present work we will refer to some of our other books, giving only the title as a reference. We therefore give the necessary bibliographical information now: *Ethics* (Chicago: Franciscan Herald Press, 1972); *Graven Images* (New York: David McKay, 1957); *In Defense of Purity* (Baltimore: Helicon Press, 1962); *Liturgy and Personality* (Baltimore: Helicon Press, 1960); *Not as the World Giveth* (Chicago: Franciscan Herald Press, 1962); *Transformation in Christ* (San Francisco: Ignatius Press, 2001); *True Morality and its Counterfeits* (New York: David McKay, 1955); *What Is Philosophy?* (New York/London: Routledge, 1990).

good, but also rejoices in doing good." Notwithstanding the fact that such a role is granted to joy (patently an affective experience), notwithstanding, thus, that reality forced Aristotle in the analysis of concrete problems to contradict his general statements, still, the abstract systematic thesis which traditionally has gained currency as being the Aristotelian position toward this sphere unequivocally testifies to a disparagement of the heart. According to Aristotle, the intellect and the will belong to the rational part of man; the affective realm, and with it the heart, belong to the irrational part in man, that is, to the area of experience which man allegedly shares with the animals.

This low place reserved for affectivity in Aristotle's philosophy is all the more surprising since he declares happiness to be the highest good, the one for the sake of which every other good is desired. Now it is evident that happiness is in the affective sphere—whatever its source and regardless of its specific nature—for the only way to experience happiness is to feel it. This remains true even if Aristotle were right in claiming that happiness consists in the actualization of what he considers to be man's highest activity: knowledge. For knowledge could only have the role of a source of happiness; happiness itself by its very nature has to be felt. A happiness which is only "thought" or "willed" is no happiness. Happiness becomes a word without meaning when we sever it from feeling, the only form of experience in which it can be consciously lived.

Notwithstanding this evident contradiction, the secondary place assigned to the sphere of affectivity and to the heart have remained, strangely enough, a more or less noncontroversial part of our philosophical heritage. The entire affective sphere was for the most part subsumed under the heading of passions, and as long as one dealt with it expressly under this title, its irrational and nonspiritual character was emphasized.

One of the great sources of error in philosophy is undoubtedly oversimplification or the failure to distinguish things which must be distinguished in spite of their having some apparent or real affinity or analogy. And this error is especially disastrous when the failure to distinguish results in identifying something higher with something much lower. One of the principal reasons for underrating the affective sphere—for denying the existence of spiritual affective acts, for refusing to grant to the heart a status analogous to that of the intellect and the will—is that one identifies affectivity with the lowest types of affective experience. The entire affective area, and even the heart, has been seen in the light of bodily feelings, emotional states, or passions in the strict sense of the term. And what is rightly denied to these types of "feelings," is unjustly and erroneously denied to affective experiences such as a value-responding joy, a deep love, a noble enthusiasm.

This misinterpretation of the affective sphere is in part due to the fact that this sphere embraces experiences of very different levels—experiences ranging from bodily feelings to the highest spiritual experiences of love, holy joy, or deep contrition. The variety of experiences within the affective sphere is so great that it would be disastrous to deal with the entire sphere as something homogenous. There is an abyss between such affective value-responses as the holy joy of St. Simeon when holding the Infant Jesus in his arms, or the contrition of St. Peter after his denial of Christ, or the love of St. Francis Xavier for St. Ignatius, on the one hand, and passions like jealousy, ambition, lechery, and the like, on the other. An abyss separates these two kinds of experiences, not only from a moral point of view, but also from a structural and ontological point of view.

We certainly find in the realm of the intellect very different types of experiences as well as great differences in the level of experience. Thus, between a mere process of association and an insight into a necessary and highly intelligible truth yawns an abyss. A reverie in which our imagination indulges itself differs from a philosophical syllogism not only in intellectual value but also in structure.

So too the realm of affectivity, embracing all kinds and types of "feelings" (the term "feeling" is thus anything but univocal), has even wider range and includes experiences which differ still more from each other.

Even the overwhelming role assigned to the heart and to the affective sphere in Christian revelation—in the notions of charity, love, holy joy, contrition, forgiveness, beatitude—did not awaken philosophy to the need for revising the conception of the affective sphere as inherited from antiquity.

It is true that there is one great tradition in the stream of Christian philosophy in which full justice is done in a concrete way to the affective sphere and to the heart. St. Augustine's work from the *Confessions* onward is pervaded by deep and admirable insights concerning the heart and the affective attitudes of man. Their eminent role, depth and spiritual character are in some way always present in his works. It even lives in his style, in the rhythm and breath of his thought and in his very voice. Yet when he speaks of the reflection of the Trinity in man's soul, it is the will which is mentioned along with the intellect and memory, and not, as we might expect, the heart. Nowhere does he expressly refute the notion inherited from antiquity, not even in his admirable refutation of the Stoic ideal of *apatheia* (indifference).

This statement should, however, in no way minimize the fundamental difference between the Augustinian and the Greek positions toward the affective sphere. Granted that Augustine fails to give to the affective sphere and to the heart a standing analogous to that granted to reason and will—although emphasizing in concrete problems the role and rank of affectivity—he likewise never accepts the Greek position of denying spirituality to the heart and to the affective sphere. St. Augustine definitely never locates the heart and affectivity in the irrational, biological sphere which man shares with the animal. So too in the tradition developing out of St. Augustine, justice is done to the heart and to the affective sphere, but only in single statements and in a general climate, as in St. Bonaventure and others. But a clear-cut refutation of the Greek heritage concerning affectivity is also lacking. (This however no longer applies to the Augustinian tradition as embodied in Pascal.)

Perhaps the most striking reason for the discredit in which the entire affective sphere is kept is to be found in the caricature of affectivity which results from detaching an affective response from the object which is its motive, that to which it meaningfully responds. As soon as we take enthusiasm, joy, sorrow as having their meaning in themselves, and analyze them and determine their value while prescinding from their object, we have falsified the very nature of these feelings. Only when we know what a man is enthusiastic about, do the nature of this enthusiasm and especially its *raison d'être* reveal themselves. As St. Augustine says, "Finally our doctrine inquires not so much whether one be angry but wherefore; why he is sad and not whether he is sad, and so of fear" (*De Civitate Dei*, IX, 5, Healey).

As soon as the affective response is deprived of the object which has engendered it and from which its meaning and justification stem, and to which it has a subservient position, the affective response is reduced to a mere affective state, which is even lower ontologically than a state like fatigue or alcohol-induced conviviality. Because affective responses legitimately claim another role and another level in the person or, rather, because they are essentially "intentional,"[1] this detachment from the object destroys their inner substantiality, dignity, and seriousness. Thus what should have been an affective response becomes something hollow, something without serious meaning, a floating feeling, an irrational, uncontrollable wavering emotion. And as soon as enthusiasm, love, joy are presented in this light, one naturally wants to escape from this unsubstantial, irrational world of "feelings" to the world of reason and clear-cut intellectual formulation. As soon as religious attitudes are detached from their object, as soon as someone sets aside the existence of God and considers him as a mere postulate for the enjoyment of religious feelings, or as an indispensable myth for man's religious needs, apart from the fatal and blasphemous conception of God here involved, religious responses are emptied of their real meaning and are desubstantialized. The great and noble reality of adoration, of hope, or the fear and love of God, so intimately bound up with the existence of God, immediately dwindles down to "mere" feeling when we consider these responses in themselves as the main theme.

Three main perversions are here in question. First, the shifting of the theme from the object to the affective response, which by its very nature has its *raison d'être* in the object to which it responds. The second perversion goes further, for the affective response in question is detached from its object, and is regarded as absolutely independent of it, as something which exists minus the object, and as having its meaning within itself. This results in a falsification of its very nature. The third perversion consists in reducing to an affective state something which is not in the affective sphere at all, or which by its very nature cannot be a feeling at all, nor anything psychic. This occurs, for example, when one makes of the liability resulting from a promise, which is an objective juridical entity, a mere "feeling" of liability. Such confusion quite naturally brings "feeling" into general disrepute, for it is a degradation and a desubstantialization for an objective bond to be reduced to a mere feeling.

Certainly, in reality, a true affective response like love, enthusiasm, or compassion need not necessarily rank lower ontologically than its

---

1. We are using the term "intentional" in the sense of a conscious meaningful relation between the person and an object. It does not mean "purposively" as in current language. We have analyzed in detail the nature of this intentionality in *Ethics*, Chapter 17.

respective object. Thus, the response of loyalty as such is no less substantial than the objective liability to which it responds. However, the
mode of existence which the bond claims to have is essentially different from that of the affective response. For by its very nature, the bond
is something impersonal and exists not like the act of a person, but
rather as an objective entity within the interpersonal sphere, independently of the fact whether the person in question feels himself
liable or not. To replace one's liability by a feeling of liability is thus
equivalent to dissolving that liability or denying its existence.
Moreover, the feeling of liability itself is also desubstantialized by this
reduction. It thereby loses its inner meaning and objective validity,
since these refer precisely to a bond which exists in the interpersonal
sphere.

Thus this reduction discredits the affective sphere doubly: first,
because one replaces with a personal experience something which by
its very nature is impersonal, and claims to exist independently of our
minds; and secondly, because it is through this reduction that the personal experience itself is deprived of its own meaning and *raison d'être*.

When certain thinkers replace the world of morally relevant values
and the objective moral law with mere feelings of sympathy, we again
have the same situation. Things which by their very nature exist independently of our minds, such as morally relevant values and the moral
law, are denied in their very existence by being replaced with feelings.
But along with this replacement there is a desubstantialization of the
moral feelings as well. In detaching them from their objects, in overlooking their response-character, one is no longer confronted with
those affective realities which really play a great and decisive role in
the sphere of morality, such as contrition, love, the act of forgiveness,
but one deals rather with mere "feelings" deprived of all meaning, a
kind of gesticulation in a vacuum.

But why should we fall prey to a discrediting of the affective
sphere and of the heart merely because of downright errors? Are we
right in ostracizing the affective sphere because every attempt to interpret as feeling things which are not feelings at all, leads to a specific
desubstantialization and discrediting of this sphere? This is as wrong
as to discredit the intellect because subjective idealism regards the
entire world which we know by experience as a mere product of our
intellect. If we followed so illogical a procedure we should have to discredit the intellect itself because of a rationalism which would reduce

religion to the sphere of so-called pure reason, as in Deism. Should we not rather refute the misinterpretations of the affective sphere, and oppose to them the true nature and real meaning of the heart?

The affective sphere and the heart have not only been discredited because of wrong theories, but also because in this realm we are confronted with a danger of ungenuineness which has no parallel in the realms of the intellect and will.

A brief survey of the main types of "ungenuineness" to be found in the affective sphere will illustrate the third source of this sphere's disrepute.

First there is rhetorical ungenuineness. This is typified by the man who exhibits a false pathos and who enjoys his indignation or his enthusiasm by inflating it rhetorically. This man has a certain affinity with the boaster. Though he may not boast in speaking about his own feats or in dramatizing events, his false pathos is in itself a continuous affective boasting.

This type has a glibness, a facility of expression, a predilection for overstatement. In imagining such a type we are tempted to think of a bearded French freemason whose voice sounds deep and sonorous when he utters phrases loaded with false pathos. This rhetorical type succeeds in producing a certain emotional "stuff" in his own soul; he may even actually experience an affective response, but he embellishes it and inflates it rhetorically. By relishing his profuse and swollen feelings, he puts himself off focus so far as any real object and its theme are concerned. This savoring of one's affective dynamism also goes hand in hand with a kind of exhibitionism, an enjoyment in displaying this pathos before an audience.

Another type of ungenuine affectivity is due to a frank immersion in one's self. This type is not rhetorical; it is not given to ponderous phrases and does not take pleasure in the utterance and in the gesturing of affective responses. But it does enjoy the feeling as such. The specific mark of this ungenuineness is that instead of focusing on the good which either affects us or which motivates an affective response, one reverts to one's own feeling. The theme of the experience is shifted from the object to the feeling occasioned by the object. The object assumes the role of a means whose function is to provide us with a certain kind of feeling. A typical example of this introverted ungenuineness is the sentimental man who enjoys being moved to tears as a means of procuring a pleasurable feeling. Whereas "being moved" in a genuine way implies a "being focused" on the object, in the sentimental man the object is reduced to the function of a mere means serving to initiate one's "being moved." The intentional "being affected" is thereby perverted into a mere emotional state which is set off or "triggered" by an object.

Yet the sentimental type does not confront his own feelings in the full sense, as the man who constantly analyzes himself does. He looks only obliquely at his "being moved," but even this suffices to throw him off focus as far as the object is concerned. Together with this structural perversion goes the poor quality of his "being moved," and of the object which evokes it.

Whereas rhetorical ungenuineness in all its various forms is mainly a result of pride, sentimentality stems primarily from concupiscence.

It would however be a ridiculous oversimplification to see all instances of "being moved" as examples of sentimentality. "Being moved" genuinely is one of the noblest affective experiences. It is a melting of one's hardheartedness or insipidity, a surrender in the face of great and noble things which call for tears (*sunt lacrimae rerum*). Only an outlook perverted by the cult of virility could confuse the noble experience of "being moved" with sentimentality. *Corruptio optimi pessima*, "The corruption of the best is the worst." The fact that the sentimental man abuses especially this experience must in no way be permitted to discredit it. Any feeling is corroded and perverted by introverted enjoyment. To be moved by some sublime beauty in nature or in art or by some moral virtue, such as humility or charity, is to allow ourselves to be penetrated by the inner light of these values and to open ourselves to their message from above. It is a surrender which implies reverence, humility, and tenderness.

The readiness to let ourselves "be moved" is as a matter of fact indissolubly connected with a full and deep perception of certain values. There is no doubt that the same sensibility and openness of heart which are the presuppositions for "being moved," are also indispensable for a full and deep perception of moral values like purity, generosity, humility, charity. Who will deny that the infinite charity of our Lord manifested in his passion discloses itself in a deeper way to the man "whose heart is moved" in contemplating it?

Time and again the Church prays in her liturgy that God may grant that we be deeply moved by the infinite love of Christ displayed in his passion and death on the cross. In a particularly beautiful prayer, the gift of tears is begged for:

> "Almighty and most gentle God, who when thy people thirsted didst draw forth out of the rock a fountain of living water; draw, we beseech thee, from the hardness of our hearts the waters of compunction, that we may weep for our sins, and by thy bounty may merit to obtain their forgiveness. Amen."

And have we forgotten the words of the bishop to St. Monica, "The son of so many tears cannot be lost." Is this expression of the heart, which is seen to be so valuable in the eyes of God, not something precious and venerable?

How wrong it is to confuse "being moved" with sentimentality is evident when we realize that this perversion is not confined to this realm alone. For it is not only the "soft" emotions which can be relished; one's enthusiasm, one's emotional heat can also be enjoyed. This introverted enjoyment can extend even to one's wrath and indignation. Needless to say, this pleasure in one's own affective heart adversely affects the genuineness of one's feeling, whether it be enthusiasm, indignation, or whatever. The indignation felt by a man who is enjoying his own emotional power is no longer a genuine indignation filled with a sincere concern about the evil against which his indignation is supposed to be directed. Through this introversion, it becomes ungenuine. The theme is shifted from the object side to the response itself, and such a shift is a death-blow to every affective response itself.

A typical form of a feeling which is ungenuine because of an introverted enjoyment is the orgy of "contrition" in certain religious sects. The cultists work themselves up into a frenzy of remorse in public, rolling on the floor and uttering wild cries. After this display of contrition, they resume their normal lives, fundamentally unchanged, but feeling much better for this emotional release of their bad consciences.

We must realize that introversion is more fatal to some affective experiences than to others. Though it destroys the genuineness of a feeling in every case, the introverted perversion is especially hideous in all religious responses. This is so because the desecration is much greater when it occurs in our relation to God or with respect to something sacred. Such desecration is seen, for example, in that very familiar form of pious self-indulgence in which prayer has almost assumed the function of a means to evoke "pious" feelings. Certain persons, for example, use their visits to church as occasions for luxuriating in sentimental "pious" feelings. The church—the *domus Dei,* "the house of the lord," of which the liturgy says, "Terrible is this place, it is the house of God and the gate of heaven"—becomes a place for emotional self-indulgence.

And, what we have already said about sentimentality, applies here also. A qualitative perversion necessarily goes hand in hand with any introverted relishing. The "pious" feelings in question are in fact not pious at all. Every truly religious affective experience bears within it something of the "atmosphere of God," of the mysterious glory of the world of Christ. Moreover, it implies essentially a deep attitude of reverence. It is impossible to make a genuine affective experience the object of introverted enjoyment. It is impossible to experience qualitatively genuine religious feelings if one approaches God not in a reverent attitude, but merely to savor one's own feelings while making prayer a means for such satisfaction. And when genuine affective experiences are granted to us, it is equally impossible to abuse them in this manner since the very structure and quality of genuinely religious feelings presuppose a state of soul for which such an abuse would be a horror.

Thus it must be stressed from the outset that it is not the affective character of a religious feeling, nor the fact that this feeling delights us, which is a perversion, but rather the introverted enjoyment of that feeling which is already, in its content and quality, a caricature of any genuine religious feeling. Such a caricature also includes the enjoyment of one's piety and, therewith, the satisfaction of one's pride.

We are far from denying that certain religious affective experiences are quite legitimately a source of great bliss and delight. To be happy while praying because our heart is filled with peace, and to be consoled because a ray of light shines into the darkness of our soul and we feel sheltered in God, are experiences which must be clearly distinguished from a savoring of certain vague "pious" feelings which are in reality anything but pious.

This indulgence in pseudo-religious feelings reaches its peak in sham contrition. Deep sorrow belongs to the very nature of contrition, and to take pleasure in it is to kill its sincerity outright, to deprive it of its substance and its depth. Moreover, the will to change one's self and to sin no more belongs essentially to true contrition. To make of contrition a merely emotional and even irrational *state*, deprived of an ardent will directed to our future conduct, makes of this feeling a sham contrition. True contrition which reaches a full affectivity implies a complete surrender to God, a falling into his loving arms like the prodigal son. Its great and solemn seriousness radically excludes any self-gratification.

We can thus clearly see why this introverted enjoyment proves to be more fatal in the case of contrition than with other religious affective responses, not to mention nonreligious affective areas.

A third type of ungenuine feeling, we could say, the classic type of "falseness," is the hysterical type.[2] We are thinking of those persons who are imprisoned in an excitable egocentricity. They may be very alert and efficient. They may have a restless energy, a peculiar intensity and liveliness. They may be refined. But everything they feel, everything they do or say, is poisoned by an inveracity and falsity. It is not only artificially heightened and embellished; it is not only corroded by an affective self-indulgence; but it is vitiated by a spirit of mendacity which, even if not conscious or purposive, infects it in its very quality.

Both pride and concupiscence underlie this perversion. These people always revolve, as it were, around themselves; they are constantly preoccupied with the satisfaction of their peculiar, restless desire to be in the foreground, to play a role, to be interesting, not only to others, but also to themselves. They may even lie when they talk about their experiences and achievements. They do not lie consciously; they are not aware of their falsehood. But the false ground on which their entire existence is built, and the qualitative lie that pervades their feeling and willing, their acting and entire behavior, manifests itself in a volubility that intermingles truth and falsehood. The burning desire to occupy the center of the stage, to make an impression on others, to render themselves attractive and, above all, interesting, impels them to say many untrue things. They are so imprisoned in this urge, and in a world in which wishes and reality are not clearly distinguished and

2. We want to stress emphatically that the term "hysterical" as used here is not equivalent to the term hysterical as often used in medicine and in psychiatry. We are thinking of a specific psychological type, a clear-cut perversion which manifests itself in one's personal life.

whose climate is one of "exaltation" and qualitative falsehood, that they do not recognize their lies to be lies. Thus they are not responsible for their lying as non-hysterical persons are.

If these attitudes help us to characterize the hysterical type, we want, however, to emphasize above all the ungenuineness of the feelings which are behind all these manifestations. What concerns us here is the intrinsic falseness of the hysterical man's joy, sorrow, enthusiasm, indignation, contrition, compassion. We want to stress this type of ungenuineness as found in these people as compared with the rhetorical or sentimental type.

The term "hysterical" is sometimes applied to an affective state characterized by a degree of uncontrollable confusion. If a man, for instance, because of the death of a loved one, is beside himself with grief and behaves with extreme inconsistency, alternately weeping and laughing, we say, he "got hysterical." If affective states such as sorrow, despair, agitation, or fear degenerate into a state of excitement which corresponds no longer to the affective response in question, the ascription "hysterical" has a certain justification.

It must, however, be emphatically stressed that there is a fundamental difference between any degree of intensity of an affective experience and the irrational, inconsistent character of certain emotional states. The person who is in the grip of these states gives expression to his feelings not only in a completely inadequate way, but by behavior which belies and contradicts the true nature of his feelings. This must be stressed because the term "hysterical" is sometimes applied to every high degree of intensity in the affective sphere. As soon as someone gives full expression to deep grief or worry, he is sometimes labeled as "hysterical," even though this response is fully adequate. The fully expressed sorrow of a loving husband at the deathbed of his wife, or the intense worry about a loved one in danger, are affective responses which obviously in no way deserve a label with a pejorative connotation. These do not possess the irrational, inconsistent character of the neurotic response, and still less do they bear any similarity with the ungenuineness of the hysterical person in our sense.

A completely wrong theory and attitude conceal themselves behind such a misuse of the term "hysterical." Many elements and false traditions have cooperated to create a mentality which deems every intense affectivity as such, and especially its full expression, despicable or distasteful. An Anglo-Saxon stoicism and puritanic prudery, as well as the unfortunate identification of objectivity with a neutral, explorative attitude (which is legitimate in a laboratory) are responsible for this discrediting of affectivity as such. Sometimes an intrusion of slogans taken from poor textbooks on psychology is contributory. At any rate, this attitude is a symptom of a deplorable superficiality.

The man who says of someone that he is "becoming hysterical" when he sees him in deep grief or in despair, or in some other profound emotion, evidences that he has fallen prey to a dangerously erroneous theory. We see how true it is when we think of one of the most sublime examples of superabundant, true affectivity: the tears of Mary Magdalene when she threw herself at the feet of our Lord. Only one who is frightened by an unwonted display of feeling, or the hopelessly neutral person who assumes the position of a mere spectator would regard as hysteria the extraordinary intensity and dynanism of a deep, genuine affective-response.

The true antithesis to a hysterical feeling is not cool indifference or an attitude which may be adequate when making up accounts or working on a financial transaction, but rather a deep, genuine affective response, a true luminous love or a holy joy.

An analogous misuse of terms is to be found with respect to the term sentimental. As we have seen, sentimentality is a perverted and mediocre feeling. To label as sentimental an intense, deep affectivity is absolutely wrong. The real antithesis to sentimentality is neither a neutral indifference which excludes feeling, nor the cramped virility of the man who believes every feeling to be a concession to weakness and effeminacy. The real antithesis to sentimentality is the genuine feeling of a noble and deep heart, such as the contrition of David, or the deep sorrow memorialized in the liturgy of the Holy Innocents: *Vox in Rama audita est, ploratus et ululatus: Rachel plorans filios suos; et noluit consolari; quia non sunt*, "A voice in Rama was heard, lamentation and great mourning: Rachel bewailing her children, and would not be comforted, because they are not."

Thus we must be ever vigilant about the free and easy use of the term "hysterical." The term is only legitimate and justified in those cases in which an originally deep and genuine affective response degenerates into a sickly disorder marked by contradictory outbursts of emotion. When it is applied to an extraordinary state of affective intensity or to its adequate, even if unrestrained, expression, the term "hysterical" is absolutely out of order. Because someone sobs or breaks down as a result of deep sorrow, he is not more "hysterical" than the inveterate and desiccated neutral who sees everything from without and is so quick with his superficial judgments.

If it is understandable that the affective sphere is looked at with some suspicion because there are many forms of ungenuineness to be found within that sphere, it is not difficult to see that this suspicion gives rise to a typical prejudice. But while prejudices are often understandable psychologically, they are no less unjustifiable.

Our brief analysis of the different types of ungenuineness has shown how wrong it is to judge anything in the light of its possible deformation. There is nothing human which cannot be perverted or falsified. And indeed we find that the higher a thing, the worse its perversion and falsification—*corruptio optimi pessima*. The devil apes God.

From a philosophical point of view, there is no excuse for discrediting the affective sphere and the heart merely because these are exposed to so many perversions and deviations. And if it is true that in the sphere of the intellect or will ungenuineness plays no analogous role, still, the harm wrought by wrong or false theories is even more sinister and disastrous than the ungenuineness of feelings. Should we look at the intellect with suspicion and mistrust because of the innumerable absurdities it has thought up, and because non-intellectual people who have never been touched by these absurdities have remained healthier than those who have been influenced by them? Is the German philosopher Ludwig Klages justified when he calls spirit "the dead alley of life" because it is the spirit—and especially the intellect—which is responsible for all kinds of artificial distortions and for the loss of genuineness in many domains of life?

No, on the contrary, it is high time we lifted the ban on the affective sphere and discovered its spiritual role. We must acknowledge the place which the heart holds in the human person—a place equal in rank to that of the will and the intellect. To see the role and rank of the heart and of the affective sphere in its highest manifestations, we have to look at man's life, at his quest for earthly happiness, at his religious life, at the lives of the saints, at the Gospel and the liturgy.

Can anyone doubt that the deepest source of earthly happiness is the authentic, deep mutual love between persons, be it conjugal love or friendship? In Beethoven's Ninth Symphony we hear the words:

Ja wer auch nur cine Seele
Sein nennt auf dem Erdenrund!
Und wer's nie gekonnt, der stehle
Weinend sich aus diesem Bund.

Yea, if any hold in keeping
Only one heart all his own,
Let him join us, or else weeping
Steal from out our midst, unknown.[3]

Can the role of the most affective of all affective responses be ignored, the love which pervades all poetry, all literature, and all music, the love of which Leonardo da Vinci says, "The greater the man, the deeper his love"; the love praised by Pius XII in the following words, "The charm exercised by human love has been for centuries the inspiring theme of admirable works of genius, in literature, in music, in the visual arts; a theme always old and always new, upon which the ages have embroidered, without ever exhausting it, the most elevated and poetic variations." And does not Holy Scripture itself say in the Canticle of Canticles: *Si dederit homo omnem substantiam domus suae pro dilectione, quasi nihili despiciet eam*, "If a man should give all the substance of his house for love, he shall despise it as nothing."

But even if one were blind to the role of love in human life, it is still true that whether one considers the main source of earthly happiness to be beauty, knowledge, or creative work, the experience of happiness is something affective, for it is the heart that experiences happiness, and not the intellect or the will.

Yet the role of the affective sphere and of the heart reveals itself in another incomparable depth and rank when we look at the lives of the saints. When we read the writings of St. Francis of Assisi or study his life, the role of contrition, of holy joy, of his "being moved" to the deepest stratum of his soul by God's bounty and by the passion of Christ, of his ardent love of Christ and of his love of neighbor, his tender love even extended to animals, cannot escape us.

Nor is it possible to ignore the depth, the spirituality, and the glory which belong only to the heart when reading the letters of St. Ignatius of Antioch, or while dwelling in the spiritual climate of the *Confessions*

3. Schiller's "Ode To Joy," translated by Natalie MacFarren in *The Choral Symphony: Last Movement* (New York: H. W. Gray, n.d.).

of St. Augustine and reading such words as, "Too late have I loved Thee, O Beauty so ancient and yet so new; too late have I loved Thee!" Or when we read the prayer of St. Bonaventure, *Transfige, dulcissime Domine Jesu*, "O Sweetest Lord Jesus Christ, I implore Thee, pierce the very marrow of my soul."

One should not offer the objection that in the lives of the saints, contrition, love, and joy are no longer affective, inasmuch as the responses in question are supernatural and not only have nothing in common with natural affectivity but even presuppose (at least on the mystical level) its silencing. Granted that supernatural affectivity differs from and surpasses natural affectivity—that it has an incomparable purity of motivation—and granted that a part of natural affectivity has to be silenced in order to make room for supernatural affectivity, it is still impossible to deny the affective character of these supernatural responses. The difference in question is analogous to the one between *sapientia infusa* (infused wisdom) and natural wisdom. Much as one may stress the difference between these, it would be nonsense to say that supernatural wisdom is no longer wisdom, that instead of belonging to the category of knowing and grasping in the widest sense, it is rather something affective or belonging to the realm of the will. The same applies to holy joy, beatitude, and supernatural love. Much as one may want to stress their difference and superiority *vis-à-vis* natural joy and love, they remain in the realm of affective experiences and do not, in being transfigured by Christ, suddenly belong to the volitional or cognitive sphere. The difference between supernatural and natural goes through all three spheres, the cognitive, the volitional, and the affective. And however much the supernatural may act in all three spheres, neither cognitive, volitional, nor affective experience loses its specific character through its supernatural elevation. The difference between the three domains of cognitive, volitional and affective goes in a completely different direction than the difference between natural and supernatural. Who will deny that Christian revelation has granted to love a supreme and central role, and that it has clearly expounded the nature of love in its full affectivity and as the voice of the heart? The words of St. Paul, *Gaudete in Domino semper: iterum dico, gaudete*, "Rejoice in the Lord always, again I say rejoice" (Phil 4:4), refer to a response of our heart and not of the intellect or will. And the role granted to the heart is evident in innumerable places in the Holy Scriptures, as for example in Christ's repeated references to joy, *et nemo tollet gaudi-*

um vestrum a vobis, "and your joy no man shall take from you," or *intra in gaudium Domini tui,* "enter thou into the joy of thy Lord." The shepherds rejoice upon hearing the good tidings; the Magi rejoice upon seeing the star which is to lead them to the Infant Jesus; the Blessed Virgin sings a song of exultation and joy in the Magnificat; Simeon is filled with holy joy in holding the Infant Jesus in his arms.

And the role of sorrow? Can one detach the doctrine of the Cross from the notion of the heart, that is, from the suffering which is obviously an eminently affective experience? Can one contemplate the infinite sea of suffering in Gethsemane and in the entire passion of our Lord and still refuse to admit the depth, spirituality, and central role of the heart?[4] If we try to conceive man as being composed only of reason and will (a contradictory notion!), innumerable passages of the Scriptures and of the liturgy are emptied of their meaning.

Instead of trying desperately to reconcile the manifest and glorious role granted to the affective sphere and to the heart in Christian revelation with the ostracism of the affective sphere by Greek philosophy, instead of getting into an impasse when we deal with the nature of love, instead of struggling with innumerable artificial and unnecessary problems, let us do away with the discrediting of the affective sphere and the heart. Let us expose the equivocation of the term "feeling" and clarify the different levels in this sphere. Let us admit that in man there exists a triad of spiritual centers—intellect, will, and heart—which are ordained to cooperate and to fecundate one another: *Cor Jesu in quo sunt omnes thesauri sapientiae et scientiae, miserere nobis,* "Heart of Jesus, wherein are all the treasures of wisdom and knowledge, have mercy on us."

---

4. In *Ethics,* Chap. 17, we have pointed out the danger of equivocation resulting from too loose a use of the term "will." We have shown that this usage of the term "will" is neither favorable to a clear understanding of the real nature of willing, nor to an understanding of the real nature of affective responses. It is indispensable to make a clear distinction between willing and affective response.

CHAPTER TWO
Non-Spiritual and Spiritual Affectivity

In our analysis of the nature of the heart, we must realize from the very beginning that the term "heart" is often used to designate man's interior life as such. In these cases, "heart" is more or less synonymous with "soul."[1] Thus our Lord says,

> . . . out of the heart of men, come evil thoughts, adulteries, immorality, murders, thefts, covetousness, wickedness, deceit, shamelessness . . .

Here the heart is not contrasted with the will and the intellect, but with the body, and especially with exterior bodily activities. It is, however, characteristic of the heart in its true and most specific sense that it is chosen as representative of man's inner life, and that the heart, rather than the intellect or will, is identified with the soul as such.

The term "heart" has had different meanings in antiquity, as well as in the Islamic and Hindu cultures. However, we are not concerned here with these various meanings.[2] Important and interesting as this topic is, our concern here is to explore the nature of the heart in focusing on a datum found in man's life, and not to pursue a historical examination of the various meanings of the term. As in *Ethics*, we want to start from the "immediately given."

1. This is especially true of the Old Testament. Yet the fact that the term "heart" is here almost equivalent to the entire soul also throws light on the character of the heart in the most specific sense. It is not by accident that the Old Testament chose the heart, and not the intellect or the will, as representative of the entire interiority of man.
2. For a study of the meanings of the term "heart" in antiquity, as well as in the Islamic and Hindu cultures, see the excellent work on this topic, "Le coeur," published in the *Etudes Carmélitaines* by Desclée de Brouwer in 1950, especially pp. 41–102.

There can be no doubt about the fact that affectivity is a great reality in man's life, a reality which cannot be subsumed under intellect or will. In literature and in ordinary language the term "heart" refers to the center of this affectivity. It is this center of affectivity that imperatively calls for exploration.

But even when "heart" is understood as representative of affectivity, it has two meanings which we must distinguish. First we may refer to the heart as the root of all affectivity. Thus just as the intellect is the root of all acts of knowledge, the heart is the organ of all affectivity. All wishing, all desiring, all "being affected," all kinds of happiness and sorrow, are rooted in the heart in this broader sense. But in a more precise sense, we may use the term "heart" to refer only to the center of affectivity, the very core of this sphere.[3] In this sense we say of a man: such and such an event really struck his heart. Thereby we contrast the heart not with the intellect and the will, but with less central strata of affectivity. In saying that something "struck a man's heart," we wish to indicate how deeply this event affected him. We want to express not only that a given incident irked or angered him, but that it wounded him in the very core of his affective being. It is this sense of "heart" which we find in the words of our Lord, "For where thy treasure is, there thy heart also will be" (Mt 6:21). In this context, "heart" means the focal point of the affective sphere, that which is most crucially affected with respect to all else in that sphere. Whereas the heart as the root of affectivity implies no special connotation of any specific depth, that is, no antithesis to more peripheral levels of affectivity, the heart in this typical sense has the connotation of being the very center of gravity of all affectivity.

We have already mentioned that the affective sphere embraces a variety of experiences differing greatly in their structure, quality, and

3. When we refer to intellect, will, and heart as three fundamental capacities or roots in man, each of them ruling over its own realm of experience, we do not claim that every experience, activity, or feature of man can be classified in one or the other of these realms. The mysterious wealth of the human being has so many aspects that the attempt to classify every human experience in one of these three realms would necessarily imply the danger of doing violence to reality. Far be it from us to yield to such a tendency which, instead of opening the mind to the specific nature of every experience, would already fix *a priori* the realm in which it is to be placed. Yet whatever may be the nature of many other experiences, these three realms play a predominant role, and we are fully justified in speaking of three fundamental centers in man.

rank, reaching from non-spiritual states to affective responses of a high spiritual order. We shall now briefly enumerate the main types of affective experiences or "feelings" in order to show how erroneous it is to deal with this sphere as if it were homogeneous. Such an enumeration will disclose in its heights and depths the tremendous role played by the affective sphere, and the place which the heart holds in man's soul and life.

The first fundamental difference in the realm of affectivity is that between bodily and psychic feeling. Consider, for example, a headache, or our pleasure in taking a warm bath, or physical fatigue, or the agreeable experience of resting when tired, or the irritation in our eyes when exposed to too strong a light. In all these cases, the feeling is characterized by a clearly experienced relation to our body. All of these feelings are, of course, conscious experiences and are, as entities, separated by an unbridgeable gap from the physiological processes, although in the closest causal relationship with them.

It is, however, important to see that the relation of these feelings to the body is not restricted to their being causally linked to physiological processes, for they also involve a conscious, experienced relation to the body. While feeling these pains or pleasures, we experience them as taking place in our body. In some cases they are strictly located in a certain part of our body, for example a pain in one's foot or tooth. In other cases, such as fatigue, they pervade the entire body. Sometimes, they are experienced as an effect of something on our body, as for instance when the doctor's needle pricks us. Sometimes, they are experienced as "events" within the body itself.[4]

Even if we prescind from the knowledge derived from former experiences and from information given us by science, these feelings clearly exhibit the index proper to bodily experiences. If we compare a headache with sorrow over some tragic event we cannot but grasp the fundamental difference between these two "feelings." One of the most conspicuous marks in this difference is precisely the bodily character of the pain which distinguishes it from sorrow. This bodily index

4. We do not need to mention instincts or bodily urges as a distinct group of bodily experiences. It is true that thirst, or any other bodily instinct, differs in many respects from typical bodily feelings, such as pains or pleasures. But they are nevertheless also *felt* and still belong, therefore, to the species of bodily "feelings." The characteristic which matters in this context also applies to them. We can thus subsume them in this survey under the title "bodily feelings."

is to be found in the quality of these feelings as much as in the structure and nature of their being experienced. This type of feeling and the bodily instincts are the only kinds of feeling which have this phenomenal relation to the body. They are in some way the "voice" of our body.[5] They form the center of our body-experience, that which most pointedly affects us and is the most awakened and most conscious; they form, in fact, the most existential nucleus of our bodily experience.

It would be completely erroneous to believe that human bodily feelings are the same as those of animals. For the bodily pains, pleasures, and instincts that a person experiences display a radically different character from that of an animal. Bodily feelings and urges in man are certainly not spiritual experiences, but they are definitely personal experiences.

This fact implies an unbridgeable gap between human bodily feelings and animal bodily feelings. Granted that some physiological processes are homologous, nevertheless in the conscious life of a human being everything is radically different by being inserted into the mysteriously deep world of the person, and by being lived and experienced by this one identical self.

In an earlier work, *In Defense of Purity*, we have dealt with the "depth" of bodily feelings in the sexual sphere, and how these are destined to be formed by conjugal love. To isolate these bodily feelings from the total reality of the human person means to misunderstand them, not only from the moral point of view, but also from the point of view of their very meaning and their intrinsic character. Only when seen in the light of the specific *intentio unionis* of conjugal love and the sanction of God in marriage do they reveal their authentic character. They display their real meaning in this function only in relation to love.

Here, it is unnecessary to say to what extent the personal character of this bodily experience shines forth or to discuss the inexhaustible differentiation of its significance in every individual person-

5. There is, however, another type of bodily experience, besides bodily feelings: bodily activities such as walking, chewing, swimming, jumping, swallowing, innervating our muscles in clasping our hands, in lifting something heavy, or in pressing or squeezing something. All these activities are more or less accompanied by feelings, but the experience or movement of these activities as such differs from feeling in the real sense of the term. We therefore prescind from them in this context.

ality. This differentiation stems from the all-important attitude of the person toward the bodily experience, from the way in which the person lives it, that is, from the difference in ethos as regards purity and spiritual integrity. But it also stems from the very fact that it is *this* person, this beloved individual personality who experiences it.

When we witness a man suffering from bodily pains which assault his body, this suffering throws into relief the dignity and nobility of the human body, a body which is mysteriously united with an immortal soul. Let us think for a moment of the terrible bodily pains endured by the martyrs! The fact that these pains were felt by persons who were ready to accept torment and death rather than deny God, and the fact that they were endured in their bodies, clearly reveals the personal character of these experiences.

And who would deny the mysterious depth of the bodily sufferings of our Lord, the physical sufferings experienced by the God-Man?

Let us now turn to psychic feelings. Here we are faced with an incomparably greater variety of types. As a matter of fact, it is in the realm of non-bodily feelings that the most disastrous equivocations centering around the term "feeling" are to be found. Many decisive differences are to be found in this realm.

An example of an ontologically low type of non-bodily feeling is the jolly mood so often experienced after taking alcoholic drinks. We are not thinking of drunkenness, but rather of a light tipsiness. This euphoria or its opposite state of depression (which may follow real drunkenness) is certainly not simply a bodily feeling, in distinction to bodily feelings connected with tipsiness, for instance, a certain heaviness. Clearly these experiences differ from bodily feelings such as physical pain or pleasure, fatigue, sleepiness, that we considered earlier. These states of "high spirits" and depression are moods which do not have the index of bodily experiences. For, to begin with, these psychic states need not be caused by bodily processes. This depression may also be caused by some psychic experience, for instance, a great tension, or undigested impression. Or again someone may be depressed or in poor humor without knowing the cause, which in fact may be traceable to a painful discussion on the previous day, or to the fact that he has been undergoing a great strain or disappointment.

But even if such moods are caused by our body, they do not present themselves as the "voice" of our body, for they are not located in the body, nor are they states of the body. They are much more "subjective," that is, they are much more in the subject than the bodily feelings. We are jolly, whereas we have pain; and this jolly mood displays itself in the realm of our psychic experiences: the world appears in a rosy light, worries vanish, and a contentment pervades our being.

It goes without saying that we do not deny that there may be several bodily feelings accompanying this psychic state of high spirits. But the fact that psychic feelings are accompanied by bodily feelings and that both coexist in us, does not diminish the difference between them. The essential difference remains even if a link between a bodily feeling and a psychic state is experienced, as, for instance, when a bodily feeling of health and vitality coexists with the psychic feeling of high spirits or good humor. Here not only do the two things coexist and interpenetrate each other, but the influence that our bodily vitality has on our psychic mood of high spirits may be given to us in our very experience. But this experienced link in no way effaces the basic difference between the bodily feeling and the psychical feeling or state.

But if states such as jolliness and depression are not bodily feelings, they differ incomparably more from spiritual feelings—for example, from the joy over the conversion of a sinner or a friend's recovery from illness, or compassion, or love. It is here that we fall prey to a disastrous equivocation in using the term "feeling" for both psychic states and spiritual affective responses, as if they were two species of one and the same genus.

A state of jolliness clearly differs from joy, sorrow, love or compassion insofar as it lacks, in the first instance, the character of a response, that is, a meaningful conscious relation to an object. It is not an "intentional" experience in the sense given to this term in *Ethics*.[6] Intentionality, in this sense, is precisely one essential mark of spirituality. The character of intentionality is to be found in every act of knowledge, in every theoretical response (such as conviction or doubt), in every volitional response, and in every affective response. It is also present in the different forms of "being affected," such as "being moved," "being filled with peace," or "being edified." Although intentionality does not yet guarantee spirituality in its full sense, it implies the presence of a rational element, of a structural rationality. Non-intentional psychic feelings are thus definitely non-spiritual. The

6.   Cf. Chapter 17 of our *Ethics* for a detailed analysis of the nature of "intentionality."

lack of intentionality clearly separates them from the sphere of spirituality.

Secondly, psychic states are "caused" either by bodily processes or by psychic ones, whereas affective responses are "motivated." Never can an authentic affective response come into existence by a mere causation, but only by motivation. Real joy necessarily implies not only the consciousness of an object about which we are rejoicing, but also an awareness that it is this object which is the reason for this joy. In rejoicing over the recovery of a friend, we know that it is this event which engenders and motivates our joy. The recovery of our friend is thus connected with our joy by a meaningful and intelligible relation. This experience differs essentially from the state of high spirits caused by alcoholic beverages, for example. Between drinking and conviviality there is a link of efficient causality only, a link which is not intelligible as such. We only know by experience that alcoholic beverages have this effect. In the case of joy over the recovery of a friend, the link between this event and our joy is so intelligible that the very nature of this event and its value calls for joy. And this means that our joy presupposes the knowledge of an object and its importance, and that the process by which the object in its importance engenders the response is itself a conscious one, a process which goes through the spiritual realm of the person. Later we shall come back to the character of intentionality and motivation.

In stressing the spiritual character of affective responses and their difference from mere psychic states, and still more from bodily feelings, we in no way overlook the fact that these affective responses have repercussions on the body. We are far from any tendency to deny the intimate union existing between body and soul. Our distinguishing clearly between bodily and spiritual experiences does not at all imply that we have fallen prey to a wrong spiritualism. It certainly belongs to the very nature of man that those spiritual affective responses have a repercussion on the body. But the close proximity of both types of experiences does not diminish their radical difference. Furthermore, we should see that even though the affective responses are able to engender these bodily repercussions, the situation is by no means reversible: the bodily processes as such can never engender those affective responses. A certain bodily state of health and vitality may be a necessary presupposition for those responses, but their coming into existence is always due to a motive, namely, the knowledge of an event endowed with some importance.

In psychic states, the "unreliability," the transitory and fleeting character which is often unjustly ascribed to "feelings" in general as opposed to acts of knowledge or acts of will, is really present: bad humor, jolliness, depression, irritation, "nervousness," have a wavering irrational character. They are the price paid for man's weakness, his vulnerability, his dependence upon his body even in his moods and his exposure to irrational influences.

It is an important task in our spiritual and religious life to free ourselves from the rhythm of these psychic feelings, not only in our actions and decisions, but also in our heart. We all know people who let themselves be dominated by these moods to an excessive degree. They are unpredictable. We leave them in the best of humor and a few hours later, without any objective reason or justification, they are either depressed or in an ugly mood. What before they had enjoyed doing, now bores or irritates them; the barometer of their soul is in constant fluctuation due to these irrational states. They refuse to do what they should do because of the change in their moods.

This does not apply, however, to all non-intentional psychic states. Later on, we shall deal with those legitimate psychic feelings and moods which are a resonance of great spiritual experiences. Far be it from us to say, for instance, that the high spirits which linger unconsciously in our soul as a resonance of our great joy over the recovery of a dear friend are illegitimate. What we mean here are the irrational moods which are not the legitimate resonance of a spiritual response and therefore are not "justified" and "meaningful," but which are the effect either of bodily causes or of experiences which in no way justify these moods. The moods either are in no proportion to the foregoing experience or are in no way rationally linked to them. The drab light in which a man sees everything because he slept too little claims, as it were, to be an authentic aspect of the world, instead of presenting itself as it really is, just as a state of mere tiredness would do, namely, as simply an effect of insufficient sleep. It is precisely the immanent claiming of these moods to be rationally justified, this presenting themselves as much more than they objectively are, which makes them illegitimate and noxious burdens in our spiritual life. This illegitimate character applies above all to psychic moods with a negative index, such as depression, bad humor, irritation, excitement, anxiety, and so forth; but it applies also to euphoric states which are not the resonance of an authentic and justified joy, but of a drug, let us say. Such moods too have this false immanent claim and are a hindrance to our real spiritual life.

It is not enough to emancipate our intellect and will from enslavement to these irrational moods; our heart must also be freed from this tyranny. When we overcome the despotism of these psychic feelings, we make room for spiritual feelings. Our heart can then be filled with meaningful affective responses. We can rejoice over the existence of great and lasting goods which deserve to be objects of our joy. We can love what deserves to be loved, we can repent over our sins, we can experience the peace and light which the very fact of God's existence and of our redemption should bestow upon our soul.

In this context, we must mention two forms of dependence upon our body, a conscious and an unconscious dependence. The first refers to the extent to which we are unable to emancipate ourselves from our bodily feelings. Some persons are completely cast down by bodily pain, or are completely absorbed by bodily annoyances or discomforts. For some people every pain, even a minor one, is a drama. Others again are absorbed in the fact that they undergo a bodily strain as, for example, when they have to remain standing for a long period of time, or have to sit uncomfortably, and consequently they are unable to concentrate on other things, to enjoy beautiful music or a conversation with a friend. Other persons, on the contrary, exhibit a great independence with respect to their body. Their soul remains free notwithstanding the fact that their body may be afflicted with pain (we are not speaking of the most violent pains). They can enjoy spiritual things in spite of bodily pains, strains, and discomforts.

Secondly, there is the unconscious form of dependence, that is, a dependence upon psychic moods which are in fact caused by our body. A person may see everything in a drab light just because he has slept too little, or he may be irritated and bad-humored because of some physiological processes taking place in his body. Here the influence of the body on our moods is not consciously experienced. In letting ourselves be invaded by such moods (which have no rational basis and are wrongly perceived as valid moods of our soul) we concede to our body a still greater sovereignty over us than if we were too engrossed in our bodily feelings. This disguised influence is a still deeper and more dangerous one. In bodily feelings the body speaks to us, we know them to be its voice. But here, feelings, though in reality caused by merely physiological processes, present themselves to us as psychic and appear to be valid moods of our soul. By taking them seriously and by yielding to them (though we should know that there is no real motive for them, that nothing has happened which would justify our changed mood), we make ourselves slaves of our bodies to a greater extent than in the former case. The very fact that this depression or mood is in no way objectively justified, that it even contradicts what we should feel as the true response to the situation in which we find ourselves, should make us suspicious of these feelings and lead us to the realization that this mood may be a mere result of bodily processes or of some repression. And this insight has a great bearing on our bad mood; it grants us a spiritual distance from it, invalidating it, and liberating us from it, at least to a great extent. Whereas bodily feelings as such remain the same whatever our position toward them may be, depression or bad moods, once recognized to be the result of bodily processes, more or less lose their impact.

Yet we must emphasize how completely wrong it would be to deny that states of depression which have a bodily cause are a source of terrible suffering and a curse for the person afflicted by them. In general, of course, these states lose much of their power over us when we are aware of their cause, when we have unmasked them, as it were. As soon as we see that the world has not changed, that nothing has happened which would justify our depression, that it is exclusively the result of a bodily condition, the state no longer has the same influence; we are in general no longer imprisoned in it; we have gained a distance from it. Nevertheless, there are cases, such as menopause for some women, or certain neurotic disturbances, wherein the entire weight of the depressive state remains, despite the fact that the afflicted one completely understands its origin. Such a one rightly seeks the help of medical doctors to remove or mitigate this suffering.

From these nonintentional psychic moods, we must distinguish the passions. The term "passion" is often identified with the entire realm of psychic and spiritual feelings, as opposed to reason and will. Traditional philosophy as well as the philosophy of Descartes use the term "*passiones*" in this sense. Yet it is misleading to use the term "passions" for the entire realm of psychic feeling. Even if one uses it in a merely analogous sense, the danger of overlooking the radical differences in the realm of affectivity remains. We should rather restrict the term "passions" to certain types of affective experiences which correspond only to the primary meaning of this term.

In speaking of passions, we may refer first of all to a certain degree of affective experience. When certain feelings reach a high degree of intensity, they tend to silence reason and overpower our free will. Wrath may deprive a man of his reason in the sense that he no longer knows what he is doing. He "loses his head" and may, for instance, furiously strike out at another person without consciously aiming at him or at anyone else. In this state he also loses his capacity for free decision. Of course, objectively speaking, he is not deprived of his free will and he is responsible for letting himself be drawn into this state. But at the same time, it is clear that he is less responsible for any action committed while in this wrought up state than he would be for the very same action performed when not "out of his mind."

In order to understand the nature of this passionate state, we must however make an important and even fundamental distinction. It is the distinction already made by Plato in *Phaedrus* between two kinds of "madness." In Chapter 18 of *Transformation in Christ* we made an analogous distinction between a "true losing of oneself" and the state of being illegitimately overpowered. We showed that there are two ways of being "out of our minds," which are radically opposed to each other, although they are both antithetical to the normal state which is characterized by the fact that we feel solid ground under our feet, that our reason clearly oversees the situation, and that our will chooses with ease.

The low way of "being out of our mind" (cited above as one meaning of passion or passionate) is characterized by irrationality. It implies a blurring of our reason which precludes its most modest use. Not only is our reason confused, but it is also throttled. Through the brutal dynamism of this state, both reason and the free spiritual center of the person are engulfed. Our free spiritual center is overpowered and one is dragged into a brutal biological dynamism. Needless to say, this dynamism is non-spiritual.

In the higher way of "being out of our mind," that is, being in ecstasy, or in every experience of being "possessed" by something greater than we are, we find the very opposite of the passionate state. When someone is moved by a good endowed with a high value to such an extent that he is elevated above the normal rhythm of his life, he also "loses," as it were, the solid ground under his feet. He abandons the comfortable situation in which his reason sovereignly oversees everything and in which his will is able to calculate cooly what he should decide.

But this does not result from a blurring of one's reason but, on the contrary, from its extraordinary elevation by an intuitive awareness which, far from being irrational, has rather a suprarational and luminous character.[7] So far from being antirational is this higher way that instead of darkening our reason it fills it with a great light. This is true although the everyday world recedes to the background, leaving the stage entirely to the immediate experience.

And far from including any tendency to dethrone our free spiritual center, far from trying forcibly to overpower our reason and will, an ecstasy calls for a sanction by our free center; it makes an appeal for this sanction. This "ecstasy" in the largest sense of the word is fundamentally opposed to any enslavement, to any overruling of our freedom. It is a gift which implies an elevation to a higher freedom in which our heart (and not only our will) responds in the way in which it should respond. It is a liberation from the fetters holding us down.

There are, of course, many stages and degrees in this affective ecstasy, but every stage is antithetical to that state in which one is swallowed by passions. Instead of having one's reason befogged as in passions, one experiences a luminous intuitive clarity. Instead of being brutally overpowered and dethroned in one's free spiritual center, one is enraptured and caught up into a higher freedom. In one case, a person is carried away by forces which are below his normal life; in the other he is transported above it by something greater and higher than he is.

It should now be clear how antithetical to one another these two experiences are. Each of them is certainly far from the normal course of life. But what is more to the point, they are still more remote from each other than from the normal state. This fact, however, is not something exceptional, for in many realms of being we encounter the same situation, namely that seemingly similar things are in fact even more remote from each other than from that from which they are both so clearly different. St. Augustine mentions in *De Civitate Dei* that both a paralyzed limb and a transfigured body are insensible to pain, but for

7. Patently, the term "suprarational" does not refer here to a supernatural light; it does not indicate the character which we ascribe to faith when we call it suprarational as opposed to the irrationality of superstition.

antithetical reasons: for these two types of insensitivity clearly differ from each other more than they differ from the healthy body which can feel pain. The paralyzed body is below the level of the healthy one, while the transfigured is above this level. An animal cannot sin, neither can a saint in heaven. But clearly this incapacity for sin is in each case something radically different. One is due to the absence of a perfection; the other to an eminent perfection. The indifference of the stoic (*apatheia* and *ataraxia*) is much more remote from the *serenitas animae* of the saint, that is, the peaceful abandonment to God's will, than to an alternatively violent rhythm of joy and sorrow, fear and hope, due to the changing events in life. One could cite many other cases in which the same truth reiterates itself.

It is of the utmost importance in our context to distinguish clearly between the two ways of "being out of one's mind." This distinction must be clearly kept in mind if we are to clarify the true nature of the passions and to distinguish them from spiritual affective responses. In Nietzsche's notion of "dionysian," for example, we find a typical confusion between true and sham ecstasy.

It must be stressed, moreover, that in the realm of the low way of "being out of one's mind," numerous different types are to be found. The specific quality of the low or negative state of "being out of one's mind" varies to a great extent according to the nature of the affective experience which leads to a blurring of reason and the dethroning of freedom. The "being out of one's mind" has a very different character and quality in the case of wrath than in the case of fear or of sexual desire. Even the "being out of one's mind" that is typical of wrath assumes a different note according to the kind of wrath in question. This is obvious since the passionate condition depends for its quality and nature upon whether wrath results from pride or concupiscence, or whether it is a "just" wrath, that is, the wrath which is motivated by moral evil.

Again the state of "being out of one's mind" has a completely different character in the case of a man who experiences unbearable physical pains or who is starving or madly thirsty, or in the case of the drug addict. Still more remote from all those forms of "being out of one's mind" is the man who, because of a deep sorrow, falls into a fit of despair, pulls at his hair, or beats his head against a wall.

Yet in speaking of passions, we refer not only to a state of intensity and violence in which our reason is blurred and our will overpowered by an intense feeling, but we also refer to a habitual enslavement by certain violent urges, for instance, when a man is devoured by his ambition or by his *ressentiment* or by his covetousness. In such cases, we do not refer to a momentary passionate state, but to a habitual domination on the part of certain tendencies. In the specific nature of this domination we find an analogy with the passionate state. This domination has an irrational, dark character, a kind of habitual overpowering of our freedom. Yet it also differs in many respects from the momentary passionate state discussed above. The domination here in question does not imply a blurring of our reason. The technical use of reason—that is, the capacity for clear reasoning and calculating—is in no way paralyzed. The man who is devoured by ambition or lust for power—for instance, a Richard III in the Shakespearian conception—has a refined capacity for clearly calculating all means necessary to the realization of his criminally ambitious plans. He even possesses a great technical self-control. Thus there is no question of a blurring of reason, as when someone does things without clearly knowing what he is doing. Moreover, his freedom is not dethroned or overpowered as in the case of the man who in his fury "loses his head." His responsibility is in no way diminished. He plans clearly and premeditates his decisions, and they exhibit the use of his free will.

But notwithstanding this, reason and will are, in this case, also enslaved by habitual passion. In a deeper sense of enslavement and at a deeper stratum of the person, the domination of a passion over reason and free will manifests itself here. Reason has become a servant of passion; its function is absorbed by the "reasonable" and efficient pursuit of the ends proposed by passion. Reason's true and ultimate mission to recognize the truth and to inquire what we should do, what is the morally right thing to do, is frustrated by the domination of the passion in question.

Similarly, free will in its ultimate meaning, that is, in its being destined to conform to morally relevant values and to their call, is paralyzed. Ontological freedom of will is, of course, neither frustrated nor even diminished. Thus responsibility is in no way lessened. The technical use of freedom in concrete decisions is also fully present: the man devoured by passion may, as we have said before, premeditate and consciously command his actions with his will. But his moral freedom is frustrated. The true use of his freedom, the "yes" to the call embedded in morally relevant goods and the "no" to morally relevant evils,

the "yes" to the call of God and the "no" to the temptation of pride
and concupiscence, is silenced by the enslavement to passions.

The examination of the passionate state has already shown us that
only certain feelings, by reaching a high intensity, will lead to the lower
form of "being out of one's mind." We saw further that even in the context of the feelings which can degenerate into a passionate condition,
the specific nature of the feeling has a bearing on the character of
"being out of one's mind." And, equally, in examining the habitual
enslavement of the person, we have seen that only certain urges,
trends, or feelings can enslave the person.

The most authentic sense of passion, however, refers to feelings
such as ambition, covetousness, lechery, avarice, hatred, envy, which
have a dark, violent, antirational character, even if they have not yet
reached the passionate stage, or have not yet assumed a habitual domination over the person. They deserve the name of passions independently of their intensity. Yet, when they reach a high intensity or when
they engross a person, they assume the most typical features of the
passionate state or of the habitual enslavement of the person. But what
matters here is to understand that they not only tend to unfold this evil
dynamism, but that in their very quality they exhibit an intrinsic enmity to reason and to moral freedom. At the same time, let us say that
while only manifestations of pride and concupiscence can have this
dark and violent antirational character, not every manifestation of pride
and concupiscence is already a passion. There is an intrinsic incompat-
ibility between pride and concupiscence, on the one hand, and a reverent value-responding center on the other. But passions in the strict
sense imply not only an antithesis to the free value-responding center, they also have the character of a wild, antirational dynamism of
an abysmal depth. (Cf. our *Ethics* for a full treatment of this distinction.)

In summary, we may say that there are four types of affective experiences which have an antirational dynamism, each in its own way, and
may thus be called passions in a wider sense of the term. First, we find
passions in the most authentic sense of the term, such as ambition, lust
for power, covetousness, avarice, lechery. All of these have a dark, antirational character.

Secondly, there are attitudes which have an explosive character,
such as wrath. We are not thinking here of the wrath kindled by ambition, revenge, hatred, or covetousness, for the wrath issuing from these

passions does not constitute a new type. We are thinking rather of the wrath motivated by some objective evil inflicted on a man, a wrath which we find "understandable." We are also thinking of the wrath which responds to objective moral evil, for example, the wrath kindled in us when witnessing an injustice. While this wrath qua wrath bears an explosive, uncontrollable, unforeseeable character, it does not have the dark, antirational, demoniac character typical of the wrath motivated by ambition or covetousness. It has rather the character of a loaded gun. It is this explosive, uncontrollable element which gives to wrath, as such, the character of a passion.

Thirdly, there are urges which are passions because of the dynamism with which they enslave the person. We are thinking of the drunkard, the drug addict, or the gambler. These urges have the character of a straight-jacket or the tentacles of a polyp; they also do not have the dark, demoniac note of the passions in the strict sense, but a gruesome, unintelligible, irrational dynamism.

Fourthly, there are affective responses which in spite of their value-response character may sweep us off our feet. Such is a specific type of love between man and woman, for example Chevalier, des Grieux's love for Manon or Don Jose's love for Carmen. When reaching a great intensity this type of love becomes a tumultuous flow which brings down all moral bastions and carries away the entire personality. In such cases, love too assumes the character of a passion, "enchaining" the lover. Yet it must be emphasized that it is both the general moral standard of the person and the fact that this love is combined with elements foreign to it which are responsible for this degeneration. Whereas the three earlier types of passions bear their poison in themselves, in the fourth it is due only to foreign elements that this type of love can exert a dangerous tyranny.

This brief glance at the affective experiences which in various ways may be called passions[8] should suffice in this context. The point at issue is the radical difference between passions and affective experiences motivated by goods endowed with values. It is imperative to lay bare this decisive difference if one is to lift the ban indiscriminately placed on the entire affective sphere and on the heart. As long as passions are used as the pattern for the entire sphere of affectivity, as

8.   Our survey of the affective sphere does not claim to enumerate all important types of affective experiences. We hope to be able to do so in another work.

long as one sees every affective response in the light of passion, one is bound to misinterpret the most important and authentic part of affectivity.

Every value-response (as well as every "being affected" by values) radically differs from passions. Is there not an abyss between a passion and the tears evoked upon hearing St. Maria Goretti's words in forgiving her murderer? And again, it is not difficult to see that the marks characterizing passion are not to be found in affective experiences such as "being gladdened" by another person's love or wounded by his hatred, nor in any value-responses, be it love, hope, veneration, enthusiasm, or joy.

It must be said, however, that notwithstanding the radical difference between a value-response (such as love, admiration, enthusiasm) and the different types of passion, we find in man's fallen nature the possibility of a sudden transition from value-responses to certain passions, or in any case to some irrational feelings. This is one of the tragic mysteries of man's fallen nature, the fact that even the noblest and most spiritual affective responses may suddenly evoke attitudes of a completely different nature. Admiration and enthusiasm may lead to an outburst of wrath in situations in which the beloved or the admired object is either not appreciated or is in some way opposed. The noble zeal to strive for justice may suddenly degenerate into fanaticism; flames of jealousy may flare up in a lover—as in the case of Othello. But the possibility of this mysterious transition in no way effaces the essential difference between value-responses and passions in the strict sense of this term.

This possibility of a sudden transition may partly explain the suspicion with which the affective sphere is traditionally regarded. One fears any affective intensity, even a noble one, because it has the character of an adventure. Later on, when dealing with the transformation of the heart by Christ, we shall see that it is only in Christ and through Christ that even a noble affective dynamism is protected from this danger of deviation.

But it would be a grave error to believe that this danger of a sudden transition or a sudden poisoning of something noble is restricted to the affective area. There is nothing in man which cannot be poisoned. Are there not analogous dangers in the realm of the intellect? There is not only the danger of error, but of intellectual pride, and of rationalism, that impertinence of the intellect which does not admit that there is anything that it cannot penetrate. *Eritis sicut dii, discernentes bonum et malum*, "You yourselves will be like gods, knowing good and evil" (Gen 3:5). Is not speculative thought a hazardous adventure? The history of philosophy certainly would seem to prove it.

If we want to avoid risk, we should have to stop living, for to live is to take risks. The very fact that God gave us freedom of will implies the greatest of all risks. If we want to avoid every risk, we should have to strive for the state of suspended animation!

We now turn back to a brief elaboration of the essential difference between affective experiences motivated by values, on the one hand, and passions on the other—a difference which, as already mentioned, is in no way effaced by the possibility of a sudden transition from one type of experience to the other.

We want especially to throw into relief the spirituality of affective experiences motivated by values. This spirituality distinguishes these affective experiences not only from passions in the strict sense, but also from nonintentional states and from appetites and urges. This spirituality also distinguishes them from a type of experience which, although intentional, is not engendered by goods having a value.

The spirituality of an affective response is not yet guaranteed by formal "intentionality," for it requires in addition the transcendence characteristic of value-responses. In the value-response, it is the intrinsic importance of the good which alone engenders our response and our interest; we conform to the value, to the important in itself. Our response is as transcendent—that is, as free from merely subjective needs and appetites and from a merely entelechial movement—as is our knowledge which grasps and submits to truth. Furthermore, the transcendence proper to the value-response reaches even further than in knowledge. The fact that our heart conforms to the value, that the important in itself is able to move us, brings about a union with the object which goes even further than in knowledge. For in love the totality of the person is drawn more thoroughly into the union established with the object than in knowledge. We must not forget, moreover, that the type of union proper to knowledge is necessarily incorporated in love. Spiritual affective responses always include a cooperation of the intellect with the heart. The intellect cooperates insofar as it is a cognitive act in which we grasp the object of our joy, our sorrow, our admiration, our love. Again, it is a cognitive act in which we grasp the value of the object.

Granted that the cooperation of the intellect in the affective value-response is presupposed, we must add that the cooperation of the free spiritual center is also called for.[9] The affective value-response thus forms a most radical antithesis to any merely immanent unfolding of our nature such as displays itself in all urges and appetites. Hand in hand with this transcendence goes an extraordinary intelligibility. The causal relation between burning and pain must be observed experimentally. In looking at the fire we cannot intuit that it will hurt us if we come too close to it, nor can we know, without experimental knowledge, that much wine will make us drunk. But this is not the case in the connection existing between the affective value-response and its motivating object. We need not observe experimentally the fact that someone is filled with enthusiasm in seeing a beautiful landscape or in hearing of a noble moral deed. The inner, meaningful relation between the aesthetic or moral value and the response of enthusiasm can immediately be intuited as soon as we focus on the nature of the value and of this response.

This spirituality of the affective value-response increases with the rank of the value of the good to which one responds. We reach a highpoint of spirituality in holy joy (for example, the joy experienced by St. Simeon when he held the Infant Jesus in his arms). In holy joy or holy love a qualitative spirituality is added to the formal spirituality which is proper to all value-responses. But although there exists a large scale of spirituality even among value-responses, all value-responses are definitely spiritual.

But it is not only value-responses that have this formal spirituality; this spirituality is also shared by our "being affected" by any good having a value—for example, when we are moved by an act of generosity or humility, or when we experience a deep peace pouring into our soul while contemplating the words of our Lord. Here we find the same marks of spirituality as in value-responses, namely, a transcendence in being lifted up by high values through the cooperation of knowledge and the sanction of our free center.

We cannot conclude our survey of the affective sphere without mentioning a typical representative of this sphere, namely what could be called poetical feelings.

9.   Responses motivated by morally relevant values call for a sanction in the strict sense of the term. But all value-responses call for a sanction in the wider sense. (Cf. *Graven Images*, Chapter 11.)

Theodor Haecker compares the realm of feelings with the sea. Indeed, feelings resemble the sea in their inexhaustible differentiations and fluctuations, especially in the realm of psychic, and not yet spiritual feelings.

We have dealt with nonintentional feelings such as bad humor, depression, or irritation which have the character of a psychic state and which may be caused by bodily processes or by psychic causes. But these feelings do not exhaust the realm of psychic and formally nonintentional feelings. There are an immense variety of feelings which play an enormous role in poetry. There are feelings such as sweet melancholy and tender sadness and vague longings. Again, there is the feeling of an indefinite happy expectation and all sorts of presentiments, and the feeling of the plenitude of life. There are also anxieties and restlessness of heart as well as torment of heart, and many other varieties of feeling.

A characteristic of this wide assortment of feelings is that they are not formally intentional. They do not respond to an object; they are not an inner word spoken to an object. Nevertheless, they have an inner relation to the objective world and are mostly linked to intentional feelings as their resonance board. They have a mysterious, secret contact with the rhythm of the universe, and through them the human soul is attuned to this rhythm.

These feelings are legitimate dwellers in man's heart. They are meaningful, and it is unjust to regard them as something unserious, or even something contemptible or ridiculous. They have their God-given function; they form an indispensable part of man's life in *statu viae*, reflecting the ups and downs of human existence—a characteristic feature of man's metaphysical situation on earth. In them a wealth of human existence displays itself. They have a deep significance and give a promising plenitude to the human heart. These feelings not only play a great role in poetry, but they are themselves, if genuine and deep, something poetic. Their subsurface but meaningful link with a world full of significance and value—a link which eludes a factual, rational formulation—gives this realm a character analogous to the one found in poetry.

Though formally nonintentional, these feelings belong, as it were, to the princely suite or household of the affective responses which, as we saw, are specifically intentional. Yet they definitely rank lower than the specifically intentional spiritual feelings.

This brief survey of the affective sphere may suffice to disclose the enormous scale of radically different types of experiences to be found in this area. We have seen the inner richness and plenitude of this sphere and the great role it plays in man's life. Above all, we have seen the emphatically spiritual character of the higher level of affectivity.

The heart, in the broader sense of the term, is the center of this sphere. The enormous role it plays in the human person discloses itself more clearly after our brief analysis of the affective sphere. Affectivity (with the heart as its center) plays a specific role in the constitution of the person as a mysterious world of his own, and it is indissolubly connected with the most existential gesture of the person and with the self. In contemplating the completely new meaning of individuality in the person as compared with an animal, a plant, or some inanimate substance, we cannot but understand the specific and significant role affectivity plays.

But there is still another basic distinction that must be made in the realm of affectivity. Apart from the various levels we have examined, apart from the structural differences concerning the ontological rank of feelings, "affectivity" can still have different meanings. In a broader sense, "affective" covers the entire sphere of feelings, and thus corresponds to the sphere we have dealt with in this survey. In the narrower sense it covers only a certain type of feelings, implying a specific ethos. The elaboration of this affectivity in distinction to affectivity in the broader sense will be the task of the following chapter.

CHAPTER THREE
Tender Affectivity

After World War I, a strong anti-affective trend developed as a reaction against the ethos of the nineteenth century. This attitude manifested itself especially in architecture and in music under the name of *"Neue Sachlichkeit,"* "new objectivity," or "functionalism." It rightly opposed the ever-decorous architecture of the Victorian epoch, but unfortunately believed that the true antithesis to this "phony" overladen style lay in a dull, technical working-out of practical necessities in architecture.

In its opposition to the nineteenth century, functionalism also invaded the field of music. Every affective element (in music) was stigmatized as "romantic," or even as sentimental. We recall hearing even a famous professor of German literature proclaim that love was a more or less petty topic in literature as compared with political problems.

But this anti-affective trend was not restricted to the domain of art; it was also found in the sphere of religious devotions. Sound as the reaction was against a sentimental and subjectivistic piety (to be found in many trashy devotional pictures or popular pious songs), here also the solution unfortunately was not sought in a genuine affectivity, but rather in a banishment of all affectivity.[1] Every stress on love, on "being moved," on longing, was regarded as petty subjectivism which had to be opposed in the name of a sound sobriety and the spirit of objectivity.

This trend is still alive today and manifests itself in manifold ways. For instance, the tendency to accelerate the tempo in music, to replace as much as possible every *legato* with a *staccato*, to interpret music full

1. In stressing this trend in the years after World War I, we do not imply that the entire epoch was characterized by that.

of deep and glorious affectivity (such as the music of Beethoven or Mozart) in an unaffective, merely "temperamental" way are all symptoms of the battle going on against affectivity in the proper sense.

It is significant that this anti-affective trend is directed against only a certain type of affectivity, what we should call "tender affectivity." The champions of functionalism and sober "objectivity" do not shun affective dynamism, or what we would call temperamental or "energized affectivity." It is not the fire of a devouring ambition or the dynamism of wrath and fury which they despise as "subjective" and "romantic." This dark, dynamic type of "energized" affectivity is accepted as something elementary and genuine.

The kind of affectivity which the "new objectivity" or functionalism fights is the affectivity of a specifically human and personal character. A cool rationality and a utilitarian pragmatism are upheld against what we have called "tender affectivity," and the expressions of a strong vitality, such as vivacity and a strong temperament (or of passions such as ambition and lechery), are not only tolerated but even welcomed as legitimate elements in life and in art. We do not imply any criticism of these passions being made a subject of art; passions have always played a legitimate and great role in art. What we are criticizing is the fact that "tender affectivity" is *excluded* from art by these champions of the "new objectivity."

No one would dream of calling feelings such as ambition, lust for power, covetousness, or lechery "sentimental." Blameworthy as these feelings are from a moral point of view, they are seen as something grand, powerful, virile, because they are not prone to sentimentality. Such is the attitude of the anti-affectivist. They are seen as something aesthetically impressive and not at all ridiculous or unfortunate.

The same applies to all kinds of affective experiences located in the vital sphere. Once again, there is no danger that one would sniff sentimentality in the pleasure someone experiences in swimming or horseback-riding or dancing.

The people who are always on the lookout for sentimentality and emotionalism direct their suspicion against the most specific realm of affectivity, namely the voice of the heart. Legitimate as their fight against sentimentality is, they unfortunately condemn the entire sphere of tender affectivity as being merely subjective, ridiculous, and soft.

Tender affectivity manifests itself in love in all its categories: filial and parental love, friendship, brotherly and sisterly love, conjugal love and love of neighbor. It displays itself in "being moved," in enthusi-asm, in deep authentic sorrow, in gratitude, in tears of grateful joy, or in contrition. It is the type of affectivity which includes the capacity for a noble surrender, affectivity in which the heart is involved.

Shakespeare's Richard III or Iago can experience the merely dynamic, heartless type of affectivity, but they know nothing about affectivity in the proper sense. In Jose's love for Carmen in Bizet's opera we still find elements of tender affectivity, notwithstanding the presence of elements of passion. But in Carmen herself we find only a heartless, energized affectivity. If we compare the ethos of the arias of Don Ottavio with Don Giovanni's "*Treibt der Champagner*" in Mozart's opera, we find in the former the specific affectivity and in the latter, the merely heartless, temperamental affectivity.

The distinction between these two types of affectivity is of the utmost importance. They differ to such an extent that the notion of affectivity embracing both is patently an equivocal one. The ethos in each case is radically different.

In distinguishing between these two types of affectivity we are not yet concerned with a moral distinction, nor even with a difference of value. For in both realms of affectivity, we find legitimate attitudes, distortions, and moral aberrations. Energized affectivity in the realm of vitality is far from embodying a disvalue. It is clear that the pleasure experienced in sports, or in a full superabundant vitality, is as such something good. The amusement experienced in an entertaining social affair is in itself something positive. This also applies to all other kinds of energized affectivity, apart from the passions in the proper sense. The satisfaction experienced in displaying one's talents and gifts is certainly something positive. On the other hand, in the realm of tender affectivity, there is the possibility of a perversion, such as senti-mentality, which is not to be found within the area of energized affec-tivity. This difference between the two affectivities is a decisive one and delineates two different realms of affectivity. In both we find dif-ferences of level, though certainly the high levels are only to be reached in the tender affectivity which is properly such.

A certain dimension of feeling which implies the thematicity of the heart is only actualized in affectivity taken in the proper sense. Although every type of love includes this affectivity, there are enor-mous differences in the degree of this affectivity according to the nature of the lover and of his love. In Wagner's unique opera, *Tristan and Isolde*, we find this tender affectivity at a highpoint. Again, we find the highest degree of tender affectivity (although in a different quality) in Leonore's love for Florestan in Beethoven's opera, *Fidelio*, and in the love duet "*O namenlose Freude.*" This is also the case in the Canticle of Canticles. The words, . . . *stipate me malis, quia amore langueo* . . . , ". . . refresh me with apples, for I am faint with love . . . ," are the very expression of this affectivity. Compare them to the merely energized affectivity of Carmen which she expresses so typically in her song, "*L'amour est enfant de bohêmes.*" The more the lover wants to dwell in his love; the more he aspires to experience the full depth of his love; the more he wants to recollect himself and to allow his love to unfold itself in a deep contemplative rhythm; the more he longs for the interpenetration of his soul with the soul of his beloved—a longing expressed in the words *cor ad cor loquitur*, "heart speaks to heart," and displaying itself in the eyes of the lover seeking the eyes of his beloved—the more will he possess this true affectivity. But to the extent that his love has a merely dynamic character and shuns a full contemplative unfolding, he possesses only a temperamental or energized affectivity.

Some people are unable to show their feelings or are embarrassed by them so that they hide them behind an apparent indifference. It is tender affectivity which they want to hide. They do not try to conceal their wrath or anger, their irritation or bad humor. They do not feel ashamed to show antipathy or contempt or excitement about their business affairs, or amusement over something comical. Sometimes they even exhibit their anger and irritation in a shameless way. We are obviously not thinking of the stoic type whose ideal is *ataraxia* (indifference) and who will suppress equally every manifestation of affectivity, be it tender or energized. We are thinking rather of a familiar type of person who is ashamed to admit that something moves him, or to express his love or to betray his contrition. However, while some people are unable to display their feelings, or are ashamed to, there are others who at times hide their feelings, not because of these reasons, but rather because of the nature of true affectivity itself. For it belongs to the nature of true affectivity that certain deep feelings are understood in their intimacy. But here the reason is just the opposite to that found in an anti-affective person. In this case deep feelings are hidden because one does not want to desecrate them, because they are too intimate. Their value, intimacy, and depth forbid one's exhibiting them before spectators. In the other case, one is ashamed of having such feelings; one wants to conceal them because one considers them to be more or less embarrassing.

Clearly, tender affectivity can also exhibit a great dynamism. But its dynamism differs thoroughly from the merely energized dynamism, for it is the result of ardor and inner plenitude. It is in its every phase a voice of the heart, never losing its intrinsic sweetness and tenderness, while at the same time exhibiting a glorious, irresistible power. It is only in the frame of this affectivity that we find real ardor. Compared with the dynamism of this true affectivity, all merely energized dynamism has the character of a flash fire.

It is true, of course, as we have already said, that this higher affectivity can be perverted. Thus sentimentality and a petty, soft egocentricity can be found only in this type of affectivity. A merely temperamental affectivity, or the sphere of passions, does not lend itself to this specific type of deviation. But to see tender affectivity in the light of its possible perversion is not only an unpardonable intellectual failure, but is also the expression of a dangerous anti-personal ethos. Here we witness something which is often to be found in the history of mankind—for instance, in the fight against religion, the Church, or against the "spirit." Though often these struggles are ostensibly carried on against certain abuses, in fact they are not merely reactions against these abuses, but manifestations of an evil revolt against high values. This remains true even if the champions leading such a fight believe that they are merely reacting against an abuse.

To see all tender affectivity in the light of its possible perversion is in reality a manifestation of a certain anti-personalism for which everything personal is necessarily "subjective" in the pejorative sense of this term. For these anti-personalists the very notion of person bears the character of a bad subjectivity, something egocentric and cut off from what is "objective" and valid. As they see it, the more personal, the more conscious and pregnant with a personal ethos, the more affective something is, the more narrow and unsubstantial it is. Against this realm of the personal they contrast forces such as instincts or economic and political affairs because these refer to communities at large, rather than to the individual person.

It would, however, be a great error to think that the opposition to tender affectivity is restricted to "functionalism," or is solely a reaction against a certain characteristic ethos in the nineteenth century. It is a mentality which we can find in individuals of all epochs and which has manifested itself in a variety of cultural realms or trends.

The anti-personalism implied in the anti-affective trend manifests itself also in an antipathy to "consciousness." Here we are not thinking so much of the fight against consciousness prevalent among the adherents of an idol of biological vitality. The adherents of this idol consider biological drives, such as instincts, to be more "organic" and genuine than any conscious spiritual act, whether an act of willing or thinking, or any affective response. The words of Ludwig Klages, "the spirit is the dead alley of life," are characteristic of this mentality. We are thinking rather of those who claim that any joy or love that is lived and experienced in a full and outspoken consciousness is contaminated by introversion and ungenuineness. We have dealt with this error in another work (*Transformation in Christ*).

True consciousness implies no introversion whatever, but rather a fuller, more awakened experience. The more conscious a joy is, the more its object is seen and understood in its full meaning, the more awakened and outspoken the response, the more the joy is lived. Tender affectivity calls for this true consciousness in a special way. The mere energized affectivity, on the other hand, does not. The anti-personalist poison in anti-affective trends betrays itself also in an antipathy to consciousness which signalizes a revolt against "self-possession," against an "awakened" being, against "subjectivity" in the Kierkegaardian sense. For the less conscious an affective response is, the less its true affective character is unfolded and the less "affectively" it is experienced.

One of the most important points in the elaboration of the role of the heart and of the sphere of tender affectivity is to expose the error of considering them as merely "subjective" or to build up a contrast between "objectivity" and "affectivity."

True objectivity implies, as we have pointed out in several works, that an attitude conforms to the true nature, theme, and value of the object to which it refers. An act of knowledge is objective when it grasps the true nature of the object. In this case, objectivity is equivalent to adequacy, validity and truth. Again, a judgment is objective when it is determined by the matter or theme in question and not by any prejudice. And an affective response is objective when it corresponds to the value of the object.

The truly affective man is preoccupied with the good which is the source and basis of his affective experience. In loving he looks at the beloved; in happiness he directs his thoughts to the reason for his being happy; in his enthusiasm, he focuses on the value of the good to which the enthusiasm is directed. The true affective experience implies that one is convinced of its objective validity. An affective experience which is not justified by reality has no validity for the truly affective man. As soon as such a man realizes that his joy, his happiness, his enthusiasm, or his sorrow is based on an illusion, the experience collapses. Thus what matters primarily is not the question, "Do we *feel* happiness?" but rather, "Is the objective situation such that we have reason to be happy?"

The truly affective man, the man with an awakened heart, is precisely the one who grasps that what matters is the objective situation and whether there is reason to rejoice and to be happy. It is in taking the objective situation seriously, in being concerned with the question of whether the objective situation calls for happiness, for joy, or for sorrow, that the great, superabundant spiritual affective experiences are engendered.

The "subjectivist" (in the negative sense of the term), on the contrary, looks at his own feelings and is concerned only with how he reacts. He is indifferent to the objective situation as such, and to its call for a response. Clearly such a man is incapable of a great, genuine, and deep affectivity.

While there is, indeed, subjectivism in the bad sense, as we have just seen, it is still true that one should wish to give a full affective response for which the objective situation calls. The capacity to make such a response is a gift, and a gift, moreover, that is experienced as bliss—as, for instance, when we fully experience happiness or love. Thus the subjective experience is a legitimate theme, but a theme that can never be dissociated from the object, which is the very *raison d'être* of the affective experience, without undermining its genuine character.

It belongs to the very nature of affective experiences that a deep joy or a deep love—while each possesses a theme of its own—is penetrated by the awareness that our joy or our love is objectively justified and objectively valid. It is thus a deplorable error to see the spiritual affective sphere in the light of subjectivism, or to believe that the cool, "reasonable" type or the merely energized affective type in whom the heart plays a minor role, is more objective. On the contrary, the affective "cripple," as well as the man entirely lacking in true affectivity, is, in the final analysis, never really objective. In failing to respond with his heart to the objective situation in those cases in which values are at stake and which call for an affective value-response, he is not at all objective.

It is high time that we free ourselves from the disastrous equating of objectivity and neutrality. We must free ourselves from the illusion that objectivity implies an exclusively observing and exploratory approach. No, objectivity is found only in the attitude which corresponds adequately to the object, its meaning, and its aura. To be neutral, or to remain noncommital when an object and its value demand an affective response or the intervention of our will, is to be utterly unobjective. Therefore every anti-affective trend is in reality sheer subjectivism because, in responding to the cosmos, it yet fails to conform to the real features and meaning of the cosmos, to the beauty and depth of the created world and its natural mysteries. It is subjectivistic, above all, in failing to conform to the existence of God, who is infinite holiness, infinite beauty, and infinite goodness.

It must be emphasized that the affectivity for which the very nature of the cosmos calls is tender affectivity and not energized affectivity. Passions, in the sense we use the word, are always subjective. And for all the other urges and feelings in the temperamental sphere, such as the pleasure experienced in sports, the question of objectivity does not arise. The cosmos calls for the tender affectivity of true love, of tears of joy and gratitude, of suffering, of hope, and of "being moved"—in a word, for the voice of the heart.

The distinction between the two types of affectivity enables us to "discover" the more intimate nature of the heart as the center and organ of tender affectivity. The elaboration of the latter has even shown us that the notion of heart as organ and center of all affectivity, such as we defined it in Chapter 2, is still too large. We must replace it by a narrower and more authentic notion, that of the heart as center of tender affectivity.

CHAPTER FOUR
Hypertrophy of the Heart

We often hear in sermons that what we feel does not matter. When speaking of contrition or of love of God and love of neighbor, a preacher will say, "You need not feel contrition or love, for real contrition and real love of God and neighbor are acts of the will." And in this context, one even hears the heart and its voice and all affective responses spoken of as being unimportant and even despicable. It has become common to say, "Feelings do not matter; love and contrition should not be interpreted sentimentally." Feelings and the heart are both classified as "sentimental," and thus excluded from the serious and important part of man's soul.

This approach is psychologically understandable, for affective attitudes cannot be freely engendered like acts of the will. It is characteristic of the affective sphere (in distinction to the volitional sphere) that it is not directly accessible to our free spiritual center. Joy or sorrow cannot be freely engendered as we can engender an act of will or a promise, nor can they be commanded as we can command movements of our arms. We can influence joy or sorrow indirectly only by preparing the ground for it in our soul, or we can sanction or disavow affective responses that have arisen spontaneously in our soul (see our *Ethics*, Chapter 25).

Since man is morally obliged to love God and neighbor and to repent for his sins, the preacher or spiritual director is tempted to deny the importance of any affective response and to replace it by an act of will. But this is done for pedagogical purposes. First of all, there is the understandable desire to soothe and allay the conscience of a penitent who might worry because he does not "feel" contrition or love of neighbor. His conscience is pacified through the assurance that if he but make an act of will and condemn his sins by turning away from them and resolving to sin no more, he can receive the sacrament of penance even if he does not "feel" sorrow.

Secondly, there is the need to prevent a penitent from believing that he is truly contrite when he only feels sorrow after sinning without firmly intending to sin no more in the future. We have already mentioned the "ungenuine" types of contrition and of many other affective responses. The legitimate desire to prevent the faithful from falling into the pit of sham contrition or sham love of neighbor makes the emphasis on the role played by the will and the devaluation of the heart understandable.

But even when the affective response appears to be genuine, the spiritual director may still be suspicious as long as the affective response—for example, love of neighbor or contrition—has not been tested. When someone feels compassion for his suffering neighbor but fails to help him by almsgiving, or by helping him in one way or another if the situation calls for it, we consider his compassion as insincere or at least as lacking in full seriousness and depth. Actually, such compassion is not necessarily ungenuine; but it certainly lacks full seriousness and depth if it does not manifest itself in actions as soon as the situation demands it. If this compassion is genuine, it is nevertheless an insufficient compassion. In order to safeguard against such insufficiency the spiritual director may stress willing and acting to such an extent that he ends by seeming to deny the importance and value of compassion as a "felt" affective response.

Understandable as the fear may be that a penitent may take his feeling of compassion as a sufficient response and overlook the moral call to action, the fact remains that compassion should be felt, since an act of compassion has something to give which no action can replace.

If a man were impelled by a Kantian duty ideal to help suffering people by efficient actions of all kinds, but did so with a cool and indifferent heart and without feeling the slightest compassion, he certainly would miss an important moral and human element. It may even be that the gift bestowed on a suffering person by a true and sincere compassion and by the warmth of love cannot be replaced by any benefit we can bestow on him by our actions if these are done without love. Certainly this compassion and love has to be so sincere and so deeply rooted in the person that it contains the full potentiality of all actions. But it is easy to see that it is completely wrong to discredit the act of felt compassion or love and to replace it by acts of will and by actions merely because, in certain cases, compassion or love is either insincere or at least insufficient. Certainly the will and actions provide tests for the depth and sincerity of those affective experiences in all cases in which an action is in question. But this does not mean that a genuine and sincere affective response of compassion is of no value. Far from it, for such a response gives something and has a value which never can be replaced by actions which do not flow out of such an affective response.

Wrong as it would be to discredit the will and actions because they are imperfect without the contribution of the heart, it is just as wrong to discredit affective responses as such merely because of the imperfection of an affective response which lacks the potentiality to express itself in actions.

The suspicion of affectivity, the whisperings directed against the heart for pedagogical reasons, can be traced to still another source, namely, the fact that the heart often usurps the role of the intellect or will. In truth, the intellect, the will, and the heart should cooperate, but each must respect the specific role and domain of the other. The intellect or will should not try to supply what only the heart can give, nor should the heart arrogate the role of the intellect or will. When the heart exceeds its own domain and usurps roles it was never destined to play, it discredits affectivity and causes a general mistrust of itself even in its own proper domain. If, for example, a man who wants to ascertain a fact does not consult his intellect, but instead claims that his heart tells him what the fact is, he has opened the door to all kinds of illusions. He has pressed his heart into a service that it can never effectively render and has allowed its improper use to stifle his intellect. Again let us consider a man who wants to know whether or not something is morally objectionable. If he fails to consult his intellect but relies completely on his heart, he may either "feel guilty" when there really is no guilt (such is the case with a scrupulous man) or he may feel pure and guiltless when he does things which are really wrong. In such cases, instead of letting his intellect decide whether a deed is morally wrong, he relies on his "feeling guilty" or "feeling not guilty." He supposes this affective experience of feeling to be a univocal criterion for an objective fact. Such a supposition is definitely wrong.

By this statement we do not intend to contradict the deep saying of Pascal, *Le coeur a ses raisons que la raison ne connait pas*, "The heart has its reasons which reason does not know." By heart Pascal means here a special form of intuitive knowledge, which he contrasts to a strict logical reasoning. There are indeed cases where we may say, "We feel this is not right," though we are not able to prove it with logical arguments. For example, in the case of a tactless remark, we feel its awkwardness even though it may not be possible to argue about it.

In stating that the heart should not usurp the role of the intellect we obviously have another notion of heart in mind and refer to completely different cases.

I once experienced a typical case of this illegitimate reliance on feelings. I was in Rome with a Russian convert. When I asked him whether he had gone to Mass on Sunday, he answered, "No, but I did something much better yet: I visited the Old Basilica of San Costanza; upon entering this church, which looks like the Grail, I immediately felt completely purified." Neither the ineffable glorification of God through the Sacrifice of Christ, nor the graces bestowed on us by assisting at holy Mass, nor the commandment of the Church to go to Mass on Sunday, counted for him. A "pious feeling," a feeling of "being purified," was considered more important than these three objective facts.

Another type of falling prey to illusion is to confuse enthusiasm about a virtue with the possession of the virtue itself. For example, a man may experience an intense and genuine enthusiasm for the virtue of obedience or humility, and thereupon believe himself to be obedient or humble. He takes it for granted that his enthusiasm for obedience is a guarantee that he is able to practice it. The illusion here differs from the more primitive illusion mentioned earlier, which results mainly from a doubtful affective experience. For when a man confuses his "feeling purified" with really being purified, his feeling purified is already of doubtful genuineness. Here, however, the enthusiasm may be genuine and is as such a first step which may lead to real obedience. It is even the basis for the acquisition of this virtue. But the illusion consists in mistaking the intensity of the enthusiasm for a sign that one already possesses the virtue one is enthusiastic about. Because one lacks spiritual sobriety, one fails to distinguish two strata of personal reality, namely enthusiasm for an attitude or virtue and the real possession of that virtue. Granted that this enthusiasm is a full and valid reality in its own right; still, as soon as it is confused with the real possession of the virtue, one falls prey to a dangerous illusion. In the final analysis, the illusion is the fault of the intellect, but it involves the heart to this extent, that the intellect wrongly demurs in matters that really concern it and allows the heart's affection to conceal the real issue. A man blinded by this illusion, therefore, would answer those who express doubt that he can really obey, "No, no I am sure I could obey a superior without difficulty, because I feel clearly that I am obedient."

Again let us say that the possibility of this illusion in no way discredits enthusiasm or any other affective response, just as willing is not discredited by the fact that sometimes the will to be enthusiastic is confused with true enthusiasm. A certain analogy to this illusion is exhibited in a general tendency in human nature to nourish the illusion that what is experienced in a convincing manner in our soul cannot change and will prove able to undergo all tests. Yet this illusion is not restricted to the affective sphere; it is a general danger and can occur anywhere. Its presence, however, does not imply the slightest taint of ungenuineness in the experience at stake.

When making a firm, free decision, a person may be convinced that nothing will be able to shake his decision. Yet afterwards he might revoke it because of fear or the pressure of other persons. Again, a man may declare that his faith is such that nothing could ever make him waver in it; yet in the hour of trial he may lose his faith. Analogously, the lover swears that his love will never diminish, and then in time it weakens or even fades away.

This is the human tragedy: the unintelligible gap between something so deeply experienced, so sincerely meant, and the actual course of life. It is the tragedy of a lack of perseverance, and it involves the saddening fact that, though things present themselves so convincingly to our minds, they may not endure. This is the tragedy of St. Peter when he says to Christ, "Even if I should have to die with thee, I will not deny thee!" (Mk 14:31). To hold the affective sphere responsible for this general weakness in man's nature would certainly be wrong.

It even belongs to the very nature and meaning of all these experiences that one has the full conviction that nothing can change them. A man whose faith or will or love did not present itself to him as unshakeable would not really believe, nor really will, nor really love. The genuine experience of these attitudes necessarily implies the consciousness that nothing can destroy them. A lover who says, "I love you now, but I do not dare say how long it will last," does not love. It belongs to the "word" of faith, to the word of a solemn and deep decision, to the very word of love to say, "Nothing could change or shake it."

And yet, though this conviction of permanence is a necessary element of faith, of a solemn decision, and of love, the real Christian is simultaneously aware of his weakness and frailty, of his instability and lack of perseverance. He knows that he can fulfill what the inner word of his experience promises only with the help of God: *Credo, adjuva incredulitatem meam*, "I believe; help my unbelief." The words of the Divine Office recited at the start of each hour are ever on his lips: *Deus, in adjutorium meum intende*, "O God, come to my assistance."

Let these two cases suffice to show us the disorder which may result from a hypertrophy of the heart—that is, from an overuse, indeed a misuse, of affectivity. The disorder arises because the heart, instead of cooperating with the intellect and the will, either attempts to replace what the intellect alone can rightly accomplish or refuses to grant to the will its specific mission. We must, however, emphatically stress that this hypertrophy of the heart or of affectivity should in no way be interpreted as the equivalent of an affectivity that is too intense. It is not the degree of affectivity which is responsible for these perversions, but a disordered state of our soul. Affectivity can never be too intense as long as the cooperation of heart, will, and intellect willed by God is not disturbed. In a man in whom the loving, value-responding center has victoriously overcome pride and concupiscence, affectivity could never be too great. The greater and deeper the potential of affectivity is in man, the better. No degree in the potential of love could ever be an evil. It is as little an evil as a great strength of will or power of intellect are evils. The greater the man, the deeper his love, as Leonardo da Vinci has said.

Far from being evil, therefore, a deep potential for love is something precious and magnificent. On the other hand, the full development of this potential cannot proceed successfully and integrally unless it unfolds in Christ and through Christ. But this necessity to be transformed is not peculiar to affectivity as such. Intellect and will must also be "baptized," otherwise they offer a specific occasion for making man a slave of pride.

If, then, a hypertrophy of the heart has its dangers, a hypertrophy of intellect and will shares an analogous fate. Cooperation of intellect, will, and heart is of the utmost importance for all three of them.

CHAPTER FIVE
Affective Atrophy

The fundamental import and value of affectivity discloses itself most vividly when we consider the danger of affective atrophy. There are different types of men in whom affectivity is maimed or frustrated. One type of crippled affectivity is due to a hypertrophy of the intellect, a kind of being imprisoned in a research spell. We are thinking of people who make every experience and every situation an object of thematic knowledge. They are incapable of dropping the attitude of intellectual analysis, and thus cannot be affected by anything or give to anything an affective response of joy or sorrow, love or enthusiasm. In these people the curiosity to observe dominates to such an extent that everything immediately becomes an object of knowledge. They always remain in some way spectators. When they see a gravely wounded man in an accident, instead of feeling compassion, instead of trying to help him, the main theme for them is to study his expression and behavior; they are absorbed by an "observing" attitude; the event is largely a new and interesting occasion for them to gain knowledge.

To the extent that this attitude prevails and pervades a man's life, his heart is silenced.

This "intellectualist" who makes everything the topic of a curious noncommittal observation, experiences affectivity more or less only in the satisfaction he derives from the appeasement of his intellectual curiosity—a poor kind of affectivity indeed! And while such a man may fall prey to passions such as pride and ambition, he is deprived of any and all "tender" affectivity. Those afflicted with this intellectual hypertrophy glide into an attitude in which every given object immediately becomes a topic of scientific or dilettante research. They fail to understand that in many situations the object calls for an affective response or for active intervention on their part.

It is easy to see that this attitude is fatal not only to the affective sphere but that it harms the sphere of action as well. Furthermore, the sphere of knowledge itself is largely crippled by this attitude. For the hypertrophy of knowledge constantly bars these people from taking a genuine interest in the object. Instead of the object proper, only the process of inquiry and research is thematic for them. The satisfaction of their curiosity, the enlargement of their knowledge is their only real concern. Now the knowledge of all objects endowed with values is thwarted as soon as the object is no longer the theme but only the knowledge of it. Especially frustrated is the possibility of any real contemplation, an attitude which implies a complete thematicity of the object (see *What Is Philosophy?*).

We can readily see the unfortunate neutralization and crippling of the personality which this affective atrophy entails. Those people do not really live who can neither love nor experience a real joy, who have no tears for things that call for tears, and who do not know what genuine longing is, whose knowledge, even, is deprived of all depth and of any real contact with the object. They are barred from all contemplation; they are cut off from real life, from all the mysteries of the cosmos.

A second type of crippled affectivity is to be found in the man who has an hypertrophy of pragmatic efficiency. In his basic utilitarian approach, he finds every affective experience superfluous and a waste of time. He scorns any deep compassion for the suffering person and declares, "Compassion cannot help—either do something or, if nothing can be done, do not waste your time with sentiment." The useful alone attracts him. In him all tender affectivity is frustrated; he knows only energized affectivity, like ambition and anger. Contemplation seems to him to be the height of uselessness, the most complete waste of time.

A still different kind of impaired affectivity which derives from a utilitarian mentality is found in the man we might call the "metaphysical bureaucrat" (cf. *True Morality and its Counterfeits*). For this fossilized "official," only those things count which have a juridical reality. His affectivity is limited to the satisfaction he feels in accomplishing everything to the letter of juridical prescription.

It is not necessary to insist on the dullness and flatness of the utilitarian affective-eunuchs of all kinds. What use do these people have for David's sorrow over the death of Absalom? What meaning can they find in the words of the psalmist, "Upon the waters of Babylon, there we sat and wept, when we remembered Sion" (Ps 136)? To understand the horror of affective atrophy, we need only compare the world in which the utilitarian affective cripple moves with the one which envelops us in reading Kent's words about the tears of Cordelia; or the words of the dying Enobarbus in *Antony and Cleopatra*, or the prayer of Gretchen in Goethe's *Faust* (*Ach neige, Du schmerzenreiche*). We need only immerse ourselves in any page of St. Augustine's *Confessions*, or hear the Lamentations of Jeremiah in the Tenebrae of Holy Week. We need only hear the words of our Lord and then turn to the world in which the utilitarian cripple lives to see that the words of the psalmist could be said of him: *Aures habent et non audient; nares habent et non odorabunt. Manus habent et non palpabunt; pedes habent et non ambulabunt: non clamabunt in gutture suo*, "They have ears and hear not; they have noses and smell not. They have hands and feel not; they have feet and walk not: neither shall they cry out through their throat" (Ps 115).

A third type of affective atrophy is that due to a hypertrophy of the will. Here the dwarfing of the affective sphere is generally something deliberate. We find it in the man who embodies the Kantian moral ideal; every affective response is looked upon with suspicion as prejudicing the integrity of his moral standard, or at least as something unnecessary. The will purposely dismisses all affectivity and silences the heart. We find it also in the stoic, who strives for *apatheia* (indifference) and sees in the suppression of all affectivity the ultimate goal of the wise man. We find it again in the man who closes his heart—seals it off, as it were—because he is afraid of affectivity. Because of a misunderstood religious ideal, either he sees all affectivity in the light of passion or else he fears the risk involved in all affection and in every "being enraptured." And so he strives to silence and ostracize his heart. Although this silencing of the heart on account of fear based on a misunderstood religious ideal is undoubtedly a grave self-mutilation, it is unfortunately often found also among pious people with excellent intentions.

When we understand the horror of affective impotency and come to realize the full import of affectivity and its center, the heart, we can see that the richness and plenitude of a man depends greatly upon the potential of his affectivity and, above all, on the quality of his affective life. In *Liturgy and Personality* we stressed the immense importance of value perception for the greatness and richness of a personality. And certainly this factor cannot be overrated. The world in which a man lives depends upon the breadth and depth and differentiation of his value perception. A man must first see the splendor and glory of the cosmos, its mysteries as well as its tragic features, its character as a valley of tears. Value perception is the indispensable presupposition for the penetration of a man's soul by the ray of values and for the fecundation of his mind. In stressing here the role of the heart and the affective life, we in no way deny the basic role of knowledge to which value perception belongs as a cognitive act. But value perception already presupposes a great and deep heart. Furthermore, if a man is to partake as a personality in the plenitude and glory of the world above him to which value perception opens the gates, it is indispensable that he be "affected" and that he respond with affective responses. A person can increase and develop all the spiritual wealth and depth to which he is called, only if he is imbued with the values he perceives, only if his heart is moved and kindled by these values and burns in responses of joy, enthusiasm, and love.

It is in the affective sphere, in the heart, that the treasures of man's most individual life are stored. It is in the heart that the secret of a person is to be found; it is here that the most intimate word is spoken.

CHAPTER SIX
Heartlessness

Heartlessness in the specific sense must be distinguished from affective impotency or crippled affectivity. The notion of heartlessness has more of a moral connotation than crippled affectivity. Yet, since it is not a purely moral notion, the analysis of the different types of heartlessness will help us to go deeper into the very nature of the heart in the most specific sense of this term.

Heartlessness refers to the crippling of a center in man's soul. Both the center and its crippling certainly possess a relation to the moral sphere inasmuch as many acts of high moral value can issue from this center only. The man who is heartless or hardhearted is incapable of really loving or of feeling authentic compassion or full contrition as long as his heart has not been resuscitated. Thus on the one hand, the silencing of the heart implied in this notion of heartlessness certainly involves the most decisive moral defects and implies as well an immoral will. On the other hand, however, the fact that the heart is not silenced or hardened does not guarantee a high moral standard, for there are many moral evils which can co-exist with a warm heart, and many other morally wrong attitudes which even flow indirectly from it. There are even specific corruptions of the warm heart with which we shall deal in the next chapter.

When, therefore, we deal with the heart that is silenced and frozen in the heartless man we are concerned not with a moral center—such as the value-responding center which is antithetical to pride and concupiscence—but with the heart as the center of true affectivity.

The heart in the narrower sense is the most intimate and personal core of "tender affectivity." Obviously the heartless man also possesses this center, only it is silenced or paralyzed in him. Hence it is of the utmost importance to understand the relation between the moral sphere and the heart in this narrower sense. We must see the various ways in which moral disorders can close up the heart.

First, the heart is necessarily silenced in any man so dominated by pride and concupiscence that morality plays no role in his life. We may rightly say of him that "he has no heart." Whether it is a Cain or an Iago, a Richard III, a Don Giovanni, or a Don Rodrigo in Manzoni's *Bethrothed*, such a man has no heart. All of these are classic examples of men whose entire approach to life is dictated exclusively by pride and concupiscence, men for whom only one thing matters, namely the gratification of their pride or concupiscence. In vain would we appeal to their hearts, try to evoke their compassion or to move them. These men are no affective cripples, as the utilitarian pragmatists are, nor are they the victims of intellectual hypertrophy; these men rather have a wild, dark and strong affectivity. But their heart is buried. Such men are incapable of love, even in the sense of a love which is at home in the realm of vital values, such as the love of a Don Jose for Carmen. They are incapable of the warmth of the *intentio benevolentiae* that every love includes. They may have sexual passion, but love is an unknown world to them. (In this regard it is very illustrative that Alberich in Wagner's *Rheingold* can attain the gold which will give him all might, only if he renounces love. Yet he is not required to renounce sexual pleasure.) They are excluded from love because love always demands the donation of one's heart, of the heart in the narrower sense.

These people are also unable to feel real sorrow. They certainly have all sorts of negative feelings; they can be torn by anger and wrath, they can be wounded like wild animals; they can be racked by the most horrible disharmony; they can be tortured by fear. But they cannot truly grieve. For real sorrow, the suffering in which the heart is wounded, implies a melting of pride, a surrender which is incompatible with their basic hardness.

But it is not only total immorality which closes up and silences the heart. Even in a man not completely dominated by pride and concupiscence, certain passions such as ambition, love of power, covetousness, and avarice may silence and harden his heart. We are faced here, then, with a second possible influence of the moral sphere in the closing up of the heart, namely, the silencing due not to complete immorality, but to the influence of certain passions as soon as one yields to them.

It is true in general that the evil offspring of pride hardens the heart more than the offspring of concupiscence. Yet certain forms of concupiscence (covetousness and avarice, as we just mentioned) also silence the heart; they suffocate it. It seems thus that some passions rooted in concupiscence are more disastrous for the heart than others. Avarice closes the heart more than lechery; the "bon vivant," even if he is greedy and impure, may still have more heart than the avaricious person. The father of Eugénie Grandet in Balzac's novel of that name is typically heartless, while Tom Jones in Fielding's novel, though indulging in lechery, has much heart.

A drunkard, for example, who is prey to his vice and who does not even attempt to overcome it, may nevertheless have a sensitive heart. He may feel compassion; he may love; he may feel real sorrow. His regrettable weakness does not necessarily close or harden his heart, as we see clearly in the case of Marmeladov, one of the characters in Dostoevsky's *Crime and Punishment*. Also the irascible man is not necessarily heartless, though irascibility may lead to terrible outbursts which momentarily silence the heart.

It is not uncommon that even people with a good heart may have a hot temper. Pierre, the hero of Tolstoy's *War and Peace*, is a man with a warm heart, capable of loving, of suffering, and of compassion, though fits of wrath do overcome him. Alexander the Great killed his best friend Clitus in a fit of wrath, but he was not hardhearted. Heartlessness as such is something habitual, a mark of a man's character. Therefore, although in outbursts of wrath the heart is momentarily silenced and even hardened, an irascible man need not be hardhearted.

A thief need not be hardhearted. Dishonesty and unreliability do not necessarily close the heart, so long as they result from weakness. All these vices, as long as they are not combined with cynicism, are compatible with "having a heart."

We should note, however, that as soon as cynicism creeps into any vice, then the vice will inevitably close or silence the heart. Whereas all vices that are the result of weakness do not necessarily silence the heart or harden it, the sinner who adds cynicism to his vices is always heartless.

In short, the second type of heartlessness can be due to certain passions which either suffocate or harden a man's heart, such as ambition and avarice. Or it can be due to any of the other passions when they are combined with cynicism. In either case the effect is the same, the silencing of the heart. The fact that certain vices do not necessarily harden the heart, however, shows us clearly that hardheartedness is not synonymous with immorality, nor is having a sensitive heart equivalent with morality.

A third type of heartlessness is to be found in the refined aesthete. We are thinking of the man who approaches the entire world from the point of view of aesthetic enjoyment. His heart is not so much hardened as it is completely cool. An iciness confronts us in such a person. When he witnesses a fire, the only thing that matters to him is its aesthetic quality. That human lives may be in danger does not interest him. He is absorbed by the enjoyment of the beauty of this unchained element at work. He remains in all situations a mere spectator. His heart is mute and deaf, cool and insensitive. He again, we may say, has "no heart."

A certain puritanic morality often leads to another type of hardheartedness, a fanatic one. These types consider the voice of the heart as a temptation that must be resisted. What they consider to be the moral law must be done regardless of the sufferings it might bring about for others. Compassion is an abominable weakness in their eyes. A striking example of this horrible heartlessness is the grandfather of Chris in William Faulkner's novel, *Light in August*. This kind of hardheartedness is even more outspoken in many forms of idealism in which the ideal is not a moral one, such as, the idolization of the state, as in Sparta. The silencing of the heart, however, reaches its climax in totalitarian states, where loyalty is permitted only toward the party. Here charity is high treason, and the heart is completely silenced.

There is still another and even more widespread type of hardened heart, namely that of the embittered man. The heart of this man has been closed and silenced not by his passions but rather by some great disappointment, a wound inflicted on his heart. This man had a heart, a sensitive heart, but the trauma he experienced has embittered and hardened his heart.

The embittered heart may be found in one who has been betrayed by the person whom he has ardently loved. It may be found in someone who has a great hunger for love, but has never met the charity he has longed for, but only humiliating indifference. Instead of being treated like a human being, he has been treated like a tool.

Innumerable may have been the trials which have had this embitter-ing effect on his heart—perhaps an uninterrupted series of misfor-tunes, or one lasting hardship, such as being crippled by an illness. Whatever the reason, this embittered heart differs from other forms of hardheartedness. It has a tragic character. It is a "hardened" heart, not a hard heart; the scars of the wound have hardened it. It is less difficult to pierce through the walls erected around this heart than those where evil passions have suffocated the heart.

CHAPTER SEVEN
The Tyrannical Heart

We have already mentioned the aberration found in the heart when it dominates both intellect and will (Chapter 4). We are confronted with such a tyrannical heart whenever the heart refuses to let the intellect decide what the intellect alone can decide, or when the heart refuses to let the free, spiritual center of the person intervene with an act of willing in the domain reserved to the will. Now we must realize that this disorder, which we have already examined with respect to the heart in the wider sense, is also to be found in the heart in the narrower sense. Instead of examining a situation with our intellect in order to know the facts and to grasp the morally relevant values at stake, instead of being eager to know what we should do, how we should respond, and whether or not we should follow the tendency of our heart, we take the trend of our heart as the only true and trustworthy guide. We let ourselves be carried away by the intimations of our heart instead of obeying God and conforming with our will to the morally relevant values at stake.

The tyrannical heart manifests itself also in a certain weakness which results from a disordered benevolence. We are thinking of people who are unable to refuse any request so long as it is not strictly sinful. When asked by a drunkard, for example, for another drink, they cannot bring themselves ever to say "no." They ignore the fact that true love compels us to think of the objective good of our neighbor and not simply to satisfy his every wish. They overlook the fact that on many occasions a "no" may be much more the manifestation of true love than a "yes." They do not understand that even though their heart should regret their not being able to say "yes" and that it should grieve that they are forced to make another person suffer, nevertheless their will should conform to the objective good for the other person.

They fail to realize that real love requires them to say no. Their weakness manifests itself as a misguided charity, not only in relation to the persons whom they particularly love, but also in any human relation.

This weakness flowing from "too good a heart" (as a misleading expression refers to it) must be clearly distinguished from the general weakness which manifests itself in yielding to every energetic influence. The man who is simply incapable of resisting any strong wish of another person, the man who is accustomed to yield to every pressure, does not necessarily have a special benevolence or tender heart. This general weakness is clearly different from yielding out of a disordered compassion.

A more serious aberration of the heart manifests itself in a certain type of injustice. A mother loves one child more than the others. In itself this would be no injustice, but it becomes so if it results in her treating the favored child quite differently, bestowing benefits on him, and ignoring the others, or worse in her making the others responsible for any naughtiness to excuse her "pet." This injustice is a result of a disordered love—or rather, an arbitrariness of the heart. There is something wrong with this love. It has an element of egoism; it lacks the character of a pure value-responding self-donation. Because she loves the child more, it seems to her justified that he alone should enjoy all benefits. Not only does she follow the tendency of her heart without checking it with her reason and without correcting it by her free will, but the love itself has only a partial character; there is an uncharitable element, a kind of self-assertion and egocentricity. This is a case of an arbitrary heart, a heart infected by pride and concupiscence.

Quite a different variety of corruption in the realm of affectivity is mediocrity of the heart. When dealing with ungenuine feelings, we already mentioned one form of this aberration, namely sentimentality. Now we want to treat briefly of various other forms of mediocrity of the heart.

One form consists in a petty egocentrism which takes very seriously every trifle that concerns one's own self. People possessing this kind of mediocre heart move in a dull and petty world; their aspirations to happiness are mediocre. Small, conventional pettifoggery preoccupies their heart. Their affectivity is shallow and out of proportion to the goods in question. Superficial items play a greater role for their heart than great and deep things.

This distortion is a caricature of true affectivity. It does not occur in the context of energized affectivity but in the one of tender affectivity. People of this sort are imprisoned in their hearts, which respond only to trifling and petty things. Theirs is a perversion of the heart, an affectivity which is deprived of all grandeur, all ardor, all true dynamism. Their heart is cut off from the world of objective values; it is unable to abandon itself; its responses do not correspond to the hierarchy of goods.

These persons are often intellectually weak, silly, and narrow-minded. But while intellectual gifts do not necessarily protect the heart from mediocrity or insipidity, neither does the absence of them necessarily make the heart mediocre. A person may have a mediocre "shallow" heart and still be intellectually gifted in a special field—even endowed with remarkable talents in this field. They may worry about trifles; they may seek primarily the satisfaction of a petty vanity and may waste their time with preoccupations about imaginary offenses. On the other hand, the simple-minded, those who have poor gifts, need not have a mediocre heart. As long as they combine with their poor intelligence an unpresumptuous simplicity and a certain humility, their heart may be free from insipidity. They may be endowed with a genuine and deep affectivity. The feeble-minded Mr. Dick in *David Copperfield* certainly does not possess a mediocre heart.

There is still another kind of egocentrism. If it is true that love is the specific voice of the heart in the proper sense, it is also true that the desire to be loved is likewise a voice of the heart. The general danger of egocentricity in man can manifest itself both in a perverted, sentimental loving and also in a disordered desire to be loved. People with this second disorder are usually hypersensitive with respect to offenses. They feel themselves constantly unnoticed, excluded, rejected, isolated, misunderstood. Their reaction to these real or imaginary offenses is not the hard, irascible one of the man who is always on the alert for his honor's sake. It is rather a soft closing-in on oneself, a gesture of retiring from others combined with self-pity.

These people are usually unwilling to consult the intellect to determine whether in fact they have been treated uncharitably. The fact that they *feel* offended is sufficient ground for them to be sure that they have reason to be offended. This egocentrism of the heart makes them "unobjective." They are prone to interpret every attitude in an unfavorable sense, as directed against them, and to consider many things which are in no way so as impolite, unfriendly, and unkind.

CHAPTER EIGHT
The Heart as the Real Self

In order to understand the nature of the heart, we must realize that in many respects the heart is more the real self of the person than his intellect or will.

In the moral sphere it is the will which has the character of a last, valid word. Here the voice of our free spiritual center counts above all. We find the true self primarily in the will. In many other domains, however, it is the *heart* which is the most intimate part of the person, the core, the real self, rather than the will or the intellect. This is so in the realm of human love: conjugal love, friendship, filial love, parental love. The heart is here not only the true self because love is essentially a voice of the heart; it is also the true self insofar as love aims at the heart of the beloved in a specific way. The lover wants to pour his love into the heart of the beloved, he wants to affect his heart, to fill it with happiness; and only then will he feel that he has really reached the beloved, his very self.

Furthermore, when we love a person and long for a return of our love, it is the heart of the other person which we want to call ours. As long as he only willed to love us and merely conformed his will to our wishes, we should never believe that we really possess his true self. Much as the conformity of his will to our expectations, his friendly looks, and the attentions dictated by his will may touch us from a moral point of view, we would yet feel that he escapes us, that his true self is not ours. As long as we feel that the benefits he bestows on us, his considerations and his sacrifices, are dictated only by a good and generous will, we know that we do not really possess the beloved, because we do not possess his heart.

If, on the contrary, the heart of the beloved is filled to the brim with longing for one, with joy in one's presence, with the desire for spiritual union with one, then the lover feels content. He feels that he possesses the soul of the beloved. But he will feel that he does *not* possess the soul of the beloved as long as the beloved only has the will to requite his love, while all the manifestations of the heart are lacking.

The heart is also the very core of the self when answering the question: Is a man truly happy? If a man only wills to be happy, or if he realizes only with his intellect that objectively he must consider himself happy, he is not yet happy. We have already mentioned that the heart alone can experience happiness. But now what we must see is that the heart here again represents the very core of the person, more than the will or the intellect do.

It is indeed a surprising fact that something which arises spontaneously and as a gift in the soul should be a manifestation of a person's true self to a higher degree than that which is an utterance of his free spiritual center. The situation we encounter in the realm of morality seems more intelligible. The word of the person, the valid ultimate word in which his self lives more than in anything else, is the "yes" or "no" of his will. His free intention, what he actualizes with his free spiritual center, is what is really himself.

When we consider that freedom is one of the deepest marks of the person, a feature in which man's character as an image of God manifests itself, and that it is here that the character of the person—of a being possessing himself—manifests itself in a specific way, then we obviously imply that it is the will which is the real self of the person more than anything else.

But this must not prevent us from admitting that in human relations, in the response to sad or gladdening events, and in all situations where *frui* (taking delight) is the theme, it is the heart which is the real self. We must not fall prey to the temptation to deduce from the very nature of freedom that what our will says must always be the ultimate word of our real self. We must instead accept the fact imposed upon us by reality, namely, that in many domains the heart is more the true self than the will. We are forced, therefore, to dig deeper in our analysis of man if we are to understand how it is possible that in many respects the heart is more the core of the person than his will.

To begin with, we must realize that the question of whether or not an experience is within the range of our freedom cannot simply be used as a measure to determine the rank of an experience. Freedom is indeed an essential mark of the person as an image of God. But what may also mark the specific high rank of a thing is the fact that it can be granted to us only as a gift.

This of course applies to the supernatural sphere in which grace is an absolute unmerited gift utterly inaccessible to our freedom. But not only here. In the natural realm as well there are many things of high rank which have the character of a gift of God. They are outside the range of those things which we can give to ourselves. All great artistic talent is such a pure gift. True, an assiduous and tireless devotion is indispensable if genius is to create masterworks, but the fact of a person's being a genius is a pure gift. No one can become a Michelangelo, a Shakespeare, or a Beethoven simply through his own striving, however great and devoted his efforts. The same applies to great intellectual talent: no one can attain the gifts of a Plato or an Augustine by his free will alone. But those gifts which are beyond the range of man's free power, and which evidence by their very aloofness man's limitation as a creature, embrace not only extraordinary talents but also the one thing all men long for: happiness. Happiness is a gift, a pure gift. Much as we may prepare the ground for it, genuine happiness remains a gift, dropping like dew upon our heart, shining gratuitously like a sunray into our soul.

The same applies to many affective experiences: deep contrition, the gift of tears, a deep and ardent love, "being moved" on hearing sublime music or when witnessing an act of superabundant charity. These experiences exist in the higher, spiritual part of the affective realm and have the character of gifts from above, just as a deep insight of our intellect is a gift.

We must understand that in the affective sphere there are two levels. The one is inhabited by feelings which rank lower than all those acts which are in the immediate range of our freedom. This is the level of the mere affective states, whether bodily ones, such as tiredness, or psychic ones, such as good humor or depression. It is the level of all passions in the strict sense, and even of many affective responses, such as those not motivated by values (for instance, joy over a financial profit). These experiences range ontologically lower than an act of promise or making a contract, or an action in the strict sense, or any work or deed.

But there is also a higher level in the affective sphere. In certain respects this level is above volitional acts, though not above the will itself. And it is this part of the affective sphere which has the character of a gift from above; this part, moreover, has the special character of being the "voice" of the heart in the narrower sense of the term. These affective responses come from the very depth of the person's soul. This "depth" must be clearly distinguished from the subconscious. It is a mysterious depth. It is not possessed by us in the way in which we "possess" actions or acts in the range of our immediate power.

Typical of man's createdness is the existence of a depth dimension of his soul which does not fall under his mastery as do his volitional acts. Man is greater and deeper than the range of things he can control with his free will; his being reaches into mysterious depths which go far beyond what he can engender or create. Nothing expresses this fact more adequately perhaps than the truth that God is nearer to us than we are to ourselves. And this applies not only to the supernatural level, but also analogously to the natural sphere.

These affections of the higher level, then, are truly gifts—natural gifts of God which man cannot give himself by his own power. Coming as they do from the very depth of his person, they are in a specific way voices of his true self, voices of his full personal being.

It now becomes more intelligible why in certain domains the heart is more the true self than the will. Yet we must add that the full voice of the heart demands the cooperation of the free spiritual center of the person.

We pointed out in *Ethics* that the deepest manifestation of our freedom is to be found in cooperative freedom. However great and admirable free will is as lord and master of our actions, nevertheless, the free cooperation with the "gifts" from above, which as such are only indirectly accessible to our free power, is the deepest actualization of our freedom, the highest vocation and mission of our freedom.

The great word in which the meaning and nature of cooperative freedom is contained in its most sublime form is the *Ecce ancilla Domini, fiat mihi secundum verbum tuum*, "Behold the handmaid of the Lord, be it done unto me according to thy word."

The highest manifestation of cooperative freedom is to be found in sanctioning—in the "yes" of our free spiritual center which forms from within our "being affected" by values and, above all, our affective responses to them. In its strictest form it is possible only with affective responses to God, or to morally relevant values. We have discussed the nature of this authentic sanctioning in *Ethics*. There exist, however, many analogies to this sanctioning in the strict sense—for example, in the "yes" of our free spiritual center in spousal love or in friendship. Again, there is an analogical sanctioning of our "being affected" by great works of art.

What matters in our context is to understand that these affective experiences which are gifts from above become fully ours, that is to say, they become ultimately valid expressions of our entire personality only when they are sanctioned by our free spiritual center. Our deep love for another person is a gift from above—something we cannot give to ourselves; yet only when we join this love with the "yes" of our free spiritual center does it have the character of a full self-donation. We not only endorse this love, but by this freely spoken "yes" we make it the full and express word of our own. This "yes" of our free center can be spoken only if a high affective experience is granted us. It presupposes the presence of a voice of our heart which is a gift from above.

Part II

THE HEART OF JESUS

CHAPTER ONE
The Affectivity of the God-Man

We have analyzed the nature of the human heart and discovered its central role in man's life. Now we shall try to delve into the mystery of the Sacred Heart. Yet we can hope to hear the voice of the Heart of Jesus, to perceive its manifestations, to grasp its ineffable holiness only if we approach the Sacred Humanity of Christ with ultimate reverence and deep recollection.

The Person of Christ is the very center of the revelation of the New Testament, for Christ is not only the Redeemer, he is also the epiphany of God. Through his Sacred Humanity he is the self-revelation of God: *quia per incarnati Verbi mysterium, nova mentis nostrae oculis lux tuae claritatis infulsit: Ut dum visibiliter Deum cognoscimus, per hunc in invisibilium amorem rapiamur,* "for the light of your glory has flooded the eyes of our mind anew in the mystery of the Word made flesh, and through him whom we recognize as God made visible may we be caught up into a love of things unseen" (Preface for Christmas). Christ speaks primarily of God's commandments, of supernatural truth, redemption, the necessity of being reborn. He speaks of what is pleasing in God's eyes, what we should do and what we should abstain from, of our vocation, of what we can hope for if we follow him. Yet every word, every parable, his every deed reveals his Sacred Humanity, and through it his divinity. And again when Christ speaks of himself as the Son of Man, of his mission, and of his being one with the Father, his words shed light on the personality of Christ and on his Sacred Humanity.

Our analysis of the nature of the heart and its role in man's life will help us discover the manifestations of the Sacred Heart in contemplating the Sacred Humanity of Christ. In several earlier works we tried to elaborate the features of the "new creature," the new morality of the saints, the very marks of holiness. The new personal world embodied in the new creature in Christ was the theme of *Transformation in Christ*, and the crowning point in *Ethics, True Morality and its Counterfeits*, and *Graven Images*. But all this sublime spiritual life, all this holy wealth is but a reflection of Christ's own humanity. We should realize also that the holy affectivity found in the new creature is but a reflection of that most holy affectivity of the God-Man himself. Now we must open wide the eyes of our souls to divine the ineffable wealth of the Sacred Heart of Jesus, the completely new quality of the affective life as embodied in the Sacred Humanity of Christ. We must guard ourselves from reverting to a familiar natural affectivity and from interpreting the life of the Sacred Heart in merely natural and even trite categories. Only by lifting up our hearts can we hope to catch a glimpse of the holy life of the Heart of the God-Man.

Step by step we shall try to gain a deeper understanding of the quality of his Sacred Heart by listening to certain of the words and parables of Christ in which this holy affectivity is made manifest. Then we shall attempt to enter more and more into the secret of the Sacred Heart of Jesus by contemplating those actions and attitudes of Christ which reveal this new holy affectivity. If it is true that every word, every parable, every deed of Christ reveals his Sacred Humanity, then there are certain commandments, deeds, and parables which have a special significance as regards the heart of Jesus—those passages in which the divine supernatural affectivity is revealed, and through that the quality of his Sacred Heart. Finally, we shall turn to the contemplation of those passages in the Gospel in which our Lord directly reveals his Sacred Heart. For indeed Jesus sometimes does disclose his Heart. He discloses the life of his Heart in its relation to his heavenly Father as well as in its relation to us. In these passages, the veil is lifted from this holy secret, as it were, and we are privileged with a glimpse of the most intimate manifestations of the Sacred Heart.

> Blessed are the poor in spirit, for theirs is the kingdom of heaven.
> Blessed are the meek, for they shall possess the earth.
> Blessed are they who mourn, for they shall be comforted.
> Blessed are they who hunger and thirst for justice, for they shall be satisfied.
> Blessed are the merciful, for they shall obtain mercy.
> Blessed are the pure of heart, for they shall see God.

> Blessed are the peacemakers, for they shall be called children of
> God.
> Blessed are they who suffer persecution for justice's sake, for
> theirs is the kingdom of heaven (Mt 5:3–10).

Those who have "ears to hear" cannot listen to these words without being drawn under the spell of the Sacred Heart of Jesus. In their supernatural glory these words illuminate the world as with a divine light. They are words so meek, and yet they unhinge the world. Not only do they disclose the path to eternal beatitude, but they permit us to breathe the odor of heaven and to have a foretaste of beatitude.

Though our Lord speaks not of himself but of attitudes pleasing to God, attitudes we should aspire to, these words reveal the Sacred Humanity of Christ in an overwhelming way, and in this humanity the very quality of his Heart. *Cor Jesu, Filii Patris aeterni, miserere nobis*, "Heart of Jesus, son of the eternal Father, have mercy on us."

> You have heard that it was said to the ancients, "thou shalt
> not kill"; and that whoever shall murder shall be liable to judg-
> ment. But I say to you that everyone who is angry with his
> brother shall be liable to judgment; and whoever says to his
> brother, "Raca," shall be liable to the Sanhedrin; and whoever
> says, "Thou fool," shall be liable to the fire of Gehenna (Mt
> 5:21–22).

A new world is opened to our minds; we hear words with a supernatural ring, as the glory of divine charity unfolds itself before our eyes. The infinite character of this charity flashes up. All obstacles and all boundaries to love are leveled. Attitudes which on a natural level seem justified are incompatible with love and even sinful. The commandment of charity reaches to unknowable depths; not only deeds positively injuring our neighbor, but even sharp words are incompatible with charity. And not only our neighbor, but our enemy also deserves charity. The reign of charity is no longer restricted in any manner or to any realm; victoriously the kingdom of charity surpasses all natural bounds. *Regnum justitiae, amoris et pacis*, "kingdom of justice, of love and of peace," as the preface of the Feast of Christ the King says.

Upon hearing these words, one cannot but be overwhelmed by the completely new quality of love which infinitely surpasses even the most noble natural love. In the face of this charity, its ineffable holiness and blissful beauty, all natural categories fail. St. John says, "This is the victory that overcometh the world: our faith." We feel compelled to add: this charity is the victory over the world.

And it is the voice of the Heart of Jesus which we hear; it is the glory of his Heart. The quality and nature of his Heart become transparent: so meek, ardent, glorious, so beyond reach of any ideal envisioned by the human mind. *Cor Jesu, majestatis infinitae, miserere nobis*, "Heart of Jesus, infinite in majesty, have mercy on us."

> But he, wishing to justify himself, said to Jesus, "And who is my neighbor?"
>
> Jesus answered, "A certain man was going down from Jerusalem to Jericho, and he fell in with robbers, who after both stripping him and beating him went their way, leaving him half dead. But, as it happened, a certain priest was going down the same way, and when he saw him, he passed by. And likewise a Levite also, when he was near the place and saw him, passed by. But a certain Samaritan as he journeyed came upon him, and seeing him, was moved with compassion. And he went up to him and bound up his wounds, pouring on oil and wine. And setting him on his own beast, he brought him to an inn and took care of him. And the next day he took out two denarii and gave them to the innkeeper and said, 'Take care of him; and whatever more thou spendest, I, on my way back, will repay thee.'
>
> Which of these three, in thy opinion, proved himself neighbor to him who fell among the robbers?" And he said, "He who took pity on him." And Jesus said to him, "Go and do thou also in like manner" (Lk 10:29–37).

The answer of Jesus to the question, "Who is my neighbor?" demolishes the walls imprisoning our heart. Again we are faced with a boundless charity, a charity limited neither by bonds of blood, nor any natural community, nor a specific affinity to another person.

He is my neighbor who is laid on my heart by God, through the special situation and its theme, even when no bond of friendship, family, or nation exists. A person becomes my neighbor because Christ calls me in him, "I was naked and you covered me; I was a stranger and you took me in. As long as you did it for one of these the least of my brethren you did it for me."

This is thrown into relief by the contrast with the attitudes of the priest and the Levite. The Samaritan's charity is not constrained by all the obstacles and reservations which confront the priest and the Levite. In them, love is kept in bondage by a natural prudence. They seem to reason, "Do I know why this man has been wounded? Do I not expose myself to all kinds of danger if I meddle in something which I cannot look into?"

Theirs is furthermore the restriction of love which consists in recognizing one obligation only, namely that of taking care of only those people who are in one way or another entrusted to us. In passing by the wounded man, the priest and the Levite think: he is neither my brother nor a relative, nor have I been appointed to take care of him; he is a stranger. I am sorry he has had this misfortune, but it is no concern of mine.

The Samaritan does not know such considerations. He hears the voice of God in his suffering neighbor. His charity extends beyond all formal obligation. Who can fail to grasp the completely new boundlessness of this love? Who can fail to sense the atmosphere of a victorious freedom in this love? Who does not taste the utterly new quality of ultimate goodness, the glorious ardor in the love of the Samaritan?

And in this charity, we also find a specific mark of the supernatural, the *coincidentia oppositorum*, "the coincidence of things which exclude one another," on a natural level. This charity is directed to an individual person. Unlike a humanitarian love of mankind, it has the character of a full interest in this one individual who through this situation has become my neighbor. It has the full existential, concrete character of true love. On the other hand, it does not have that exclusiveness which all other categories of love mor or less possess. It will embrace everyone as soon as, through some situation, he becomes my neighbor, *proximus*. And thus we find in this love of neighbor an interpenetration of the full existential individual character of love with an all-embracing breadth.

This love differs completely from the mere natural benevolence of the man who, because of his "good heart," is ready to help other people and to yield to their wishes. Attractive as this benevolence may be, it is separated from charity by an abyss. Natural benevolence sees in the other person simply a human being. Charity, on the other hand, pierces through to the incomparable value of a personal being destined to love God and to be united with him. It sees the image of God in him—this individual loved by Christ and for whom Christ died on the Cross. This love transcends the natural realm by its very quality; in it we are lifted up into the world of Christ where a view of the neighbor is granted to us in the glorious *lumen Christi*, "light of Christ."

Cor Jesu, bonitate et amore plenum, miserere nobis, "Heart of Jesus, full of kindness and love, have mercy on us."

> And on the third day a marriage took place at Cana of Galilee, and the mother of Jesus was there. Now Jesus too was invited to the marriage, and also his disciples. And the wine having run short, the mother of Jesus said to him, "They have no wine." And Jesus said to her, "What wouldst thou have me do, woman? My hour has not yet come." His mother said to the attendants, "Do whatever he tells you."
>
> Now six stone water-jars were placed there, after the Jewish manner of purification, each holding two or three measures. Jesus said to them, "Fill the jars with water." And they filled them to the brim. And Jesus said to them, "Draw out now, and take to the chief steward." And they took it to him.
>
> Now when the chief steward had tasted the water after it had become wine, not knowing whence it was (though the attendants who had drawn the water knew), the chief steward called the bridegroom, and said to him, "Every man at first sets forth the good wine, and when they have drunk freely, then that which is poorer. But thou hast kept the good wine until now."
>
> This first of his signs Jesus worked at Cana of Galilee; and he manifested his glory, and his disciples believed in him (Jn 2:1–11).

The first miracle of our Lord at the wedding of Cana is one of the three mysteries of the feast of Epiphany. The Gospel says: "He manifested his glory, and his disciples believed in him." In this miracle the Church primarily sees the manifestation of the divinity of Christ. Yet, it also is a revelation of the boundless superabundance of divine love. The first miracle of Christ was neither the healing of the sick, nor the restoration of a natural good—like sight to the blind—nor even an indispensable good like the multiplication of the loaves. The transmutation of water into wine was not an indispensable good either for the couple or for the wedding as such. It served merely to heighten the joy of the feast. It was not even absolutely lacking, but was only in insufficient quantity. Divine superabundance! Christ our Redeemer, who continually exhorts us to seek only the one thing necessary, manifests such an interest that the wedding should take place in cloudless joy, that the bridegroom should not be humiliated or perturbed by the insufficiency of wine!

Divine, boundless superabundance of love! What an abyss separates it from the hard zeal of many pious people who are moved and interested only when either something vital to their neighbor's eternal welfare or at least some elementary indispensable good is at stake. That the wine was not sufficient for a wedding would strike those "pious souls" as a trifle not deserving their attention. They forget that the sublime words of St. Aloysius, *Quid ad aeternitatem?* "What is this to eternity?" should be applied to one's own person only, but never to one's neighbor.

Certainly our neighbor's eternal welfare should not only be our first consideration but should so concern us in our acts of charity that no good should be bestowed on a person which might endanger his salvation. But the question of whether something serves his eternal welfare should not limit the flow of our charity. Many pious persons mistakenly believe that piety requires that they limit their interest in the welfare of their neighbor either to those goods which are pertinent to their eternal welfare or which are indispensable earthly goods. Their charity is cool, calculated, and marked by a utilitarian dryness. An abyss yawns between their puritan, parsimonious, and moralistic charity and Christ's superabundance of charity as evidenced in this miracle at the wedding of Cana. Here we find this divine extravagance, this unlimitedness of charity which reaches to the smallest detail. It is this divine tenderness which excludes no gift from its intention as long as it is a beneficial good to the person, ranging from the highest to the merely legitimately agreeable goods. Indeed the miracle at Cana allows us a glance into the tenderness, differentiation, and superabundance of the charity of Christ: our Lord deigns to intervene with a miracle to provide a wedding with sufficient wine. This charity of our Lord, which implies attention to what seems a trifle, in no way contradicts the challenge to strive first for the *unum necessarium*, "the one thing necessary." At Cana, joy was the theme. At every feast and in particular at a feast celebrating a wedding, joy is the theme. Wine was a symbol of this joyful celebration and thus a sufficiency of wine, though not indispensable, assumed a thematic character. In cases in which another theme is at stake, our Lord may have chided those who were worrying over such a trifle.

In delving into the divine superabundance of this charity filled with the most delicate tenderness, the Sacred Heart of Jesus discloses itself more and more in its quality. *Cor Jesu, fornax ardens caritatis, miserere nobis*, "Heart of Jesus, glowing furnace of charity, have mercy on us."

We could never really grasp the nature of the charity dwelling in the heart of the God-Man if we did not first immerse ourselves into the great mystery of mercy, the breath of which pervades the entire revelation of Christ and the light of which dispels the shadow of death.

Every word spoken by Christ breathes a supernatural, divine atmosphere. Whenever a human mind tries to ascend to God, it is bound to remain in the realm of the abstract if it wants to avoid anthropomorphism. The concrete divine world is accessible only when God speaks to us in revelation. Thus when Christ uses human comparisons in parables, when he refers to classical features of our earthly life, these parables nevertheless breathe a glorious, divine atmosphere. They represent the utmost antithesis to any anthropomorphism. The human, natural examples as used by Christ become transparent to the world above. We experience the breath of the supernatural world in all its concreteness; a light from above shines into our minds upon hearing his words. It is an analogy to the epiphany of God in Christ's Sacred Humanity; it is a reflection of the mystery of the Incarnation. Every word of Christ, every parable, shares in some way in the mystery of the Word made flesh, from whose "brightness a new light hath risen to shine on the eyes of our souls."

This is the very reverse of the process of anthropomorphism. In anthropomorphism God is drawn down into human categories. The attempt to ascend concretely to God ends not only in our being thrown back into a completely finite earthly realm, but into a distorted earthly realm, an oppressing finiteness.

The finite—as long as it is seen as finite—is rich in beauty and delight. But when one projects finite categories into the absolute or, conversely, when one tries to press the absolute into finite categories, one feels choked, as it were, and experiences the stifling character of anthropomorphism.

In Christ's parables, on the contrary, well-known human situations become a window into the true heavenly world and enable us to experience the mysterious glory of "the things above," the things of which St. Paul says, *quae sursum sunt sapite*, "seek the things that are above." They draw us up and immerse us into the very fullness of the divine.

And, as mentioned above, in every word spoken by Christ, in every commandment and every parable, the Sacred Humanity of Christ manifests itself and through the Sacred Humanity, the Word.

> And he said, "A certain man had two sons. And the younger of them said to his father, 'Father, give me the share of the property that falls to me.' And he divided his means between them.
>
> And not many days later, the younger son gathered up all his wealth, and took his journey into a far country; and there he squandered his fortune in loose living. And after he had spent all, there came a grievous famine over that country, and he began himself to suffer want. And he went and joined one of the citizens of that country, who sent him to his farm to feed swine. And he longed to fill himself with the pods that the swine were eating, but no one offered to give them to him.
>
> But when he came to himself, he said, 'How many hired men in my father's house have bread in abundance, while I am perishing here with hunger! I will get up and go to my father and will say to him, Father, I have sinned against heaven and before thee. I am no longer worthy to be called thy son; make me as one of thy hired men.' And he arose and went to his father.
>
> But while he was yet a long way off, his father saw him and was moved with compassion, and ran and fell upon his neck and kissed him. And the son said to him, 'Father, I have sinned against heaven and before thee. I am no longer worthy to be called thy son.' But the father said to his servants, 'Fetch quickly the best robe and put it on him, and give him a ring for his finger and sandals for his feet; and bring out the fattened calf and kill it, and let us eat and make merry; and because this my son was dead, and has come to life again; he was lost, and is found.' And they began to make merry.

Now his elder son was in the field; and as he came and drew near to the house, he heard music and dancing. And calling one of the servants he inquired what this meant. And he said to him, 'Thy brother has come, and thy father has killed the fattened calf, because he has got him back safe.' But he was angered and would not go in. His father, therefore, came out and began to entreat him. But he answered and said to his father, 'Behold these many years I have been serving thee, and have never transgressed one of thy commands; and yet thou hast never given me a kid that I might make merry with my friends. But when this thy son comes, who has devoured his means with harlots, thou hast killed for him the fattened calf.'

But he said to him, 'Son, thou art always with me, and all that is mine is thine; but we were bound to make merry and rejoice, for this thy brother was dead, and has come to life; he was lost, and is found (Lk 15:11–32).

While reading the parable of the prodigal son our soul is touched by the breath of divine mercy. We grasp the victorious redeeming flow of God's mercy, the reversal of human categories of justice. This parable also reveals the unique nature and incomparable role of contrition. Indeed the words of the father, "because this my son was dead and has come to life again," express the resurrection of the soul which takes place in contrition. The comparison of the two brothers—the repentant sinner and the "just" one—shows us the mysterious depths into which contrition leads men. In the one, we find the unique confrontation with God embodied in contrition, its liberating breath, its unique breakthrough; in the other, the limitedness and pettiness of the "just" one who believes himself a fruitful and good servant. The words of the prodigal son, "I am no longer worthy to be called thy son; make me as one of thy hired men," reveal the humility which true contrition implies.

Divine mercy and man's contrition are mysteriously linked; they correspond to each other. In true contrition, there is a reflection of divine mercy and an inner qualitative affinity. For if contrition is essentially the act of a human person, it is nevertheless only possible as a response to God in the soul of the man who is touched by God. True contrition appeals to God's mercy. The repentant sinner realizes that he does not deserve mercy, that he must humble himself, but nonetheless he pleads for it, "But when he came to himself, he said, 'How many hired men in my father's house have bread in abundance, while I am perishing here in hunger! I will get up and go to my father, and will say to him, Father, I have sinned against heaven and before thee.'"

But the father's mercy anticipated even the manifestation of the prodigal son's contrition, his begging for forgiveness. Upon seeing him from afar, he himself went to meet him, to receive him into his loving arms. And far from fulfilling only what the son asks of him, he receives him lovingly as a son and kills the fattened calf in order to celebrate the great feast of his conversion. We hear the answer given to the older brother, "Son thou art always with me, and all that is mine is thine; but we were bound to make merry and rejoice, for this thy brother was dead, and has come to life; he was lost, and is found." We are transported into the glory of the Gospel, the *euangelion*, "the good news." The light of divine mercy lifts our souls. The inexhaustible wealth of the parable of the prodigal son immerses us in the mystery of redemption. And this parable also is pervaded by the new, transfigured affectivity, the holy affectivity dwelling in the Sacred Heart of Jesus: *Cor Jesu, desiderium collium aeternorum, miserere nobis*, "Heart of Jesus, desire of the eternal hills, have mercy on us."

> Now one of the Pharisees asked him to dine with him; so he went into the house of the Pharisee and reclined at table. And behold, a woman in the town who was a sinner, upon learning that he was at table in the Pharisee's house, brought an alabaster jar of ointment; and standing behind him at his feet, she began to bathe his feet with her tears, and wiped them with the hair of her head, and kissed his feet, and anointed them with ointment.
>
> Now when the Pharisee, who had invited him, saw it, he said to himself, "This man, were he a prophet, would surely know who and what manner of woman this is who is touching him, for she is a sinner."
>
> And Jesus answered and said to him, "Simon, I have something to say to thee." And he said, "Master, speak." "A certain moneylender had two debtors; the one owed five hundred denarii, the other fifty. As they had no means of paying, he forgave them both. Which of them, therefore, will love him

more?" Simon answered and said, "He, I suppose, to whom he
forgave more." And he said to him, "Thou hast judged rightly." And turning to the woman, he said to Simon, "Dost thou
see this woman? I came into thy house; thou gavest me no
water for my feet; but she has bathed my feet with tears, and
has wiped them with her hair. Thou gavest me no kiss; but she,
from the moment she entered, has not ceased to kiss my feet.
Thou didst not anoint my head with oil; but she has anointed
my feet with ointment. Wherefore I say to thee, her sins, many
as they are, shall be forgiven her, because she has loved much.
But he to whom little is forgiven, loves little." And he said to
her, "Thy sins are forgiven." And they who were at table with
him began to say within themselves, "Who is this man, who
even forgives sins?" But he said to the woman, "Thy faith has
saved thee; go in peace" (Lk 7:36–50).

The mercy of God is the source of all our hope. We live on God's
mercy. The entire Old Testament is pervaded by the appeal to God's
mercy and by the faith that God will grant his mercy to the repentant
sinner and that he will restore his soul:

> *Miserere mei, Deus, secundum magnam misericordiam tuam.*
> "Have mercy on me, O God, according to Thy great mercy."

> *Asperges me hyssopo et mundabor . . .*
> "Thou shalt sprinkle me with hyssop, and I shall be
> cleansed. . . ."

But what lives as hope in the Old Covenant finds its fulfillment in
Christ. Christ is the Incarnate Mercy, and in his attitude toward Mary
Magdalene, the full glory of God's infinite mercy is embodied. The
drama of fallen man and the infinitely Holy God displays itself before
our minds. The contrition of Mary Magdalene is an epitome of all true
and ardent contrition. And every manifestation of her contrition as
enumerated by our Lord breathes her ardent love for him. Jesus refers
to them as though they expressed the degree of her love. We hear
those words of unfathomable depth resplendent with the primacy of
love, "Her sins . . . shall be forgiven her, because she has loved much."
It is the great banquet of divine mercy, the display of the condescending divine charity; Jesus, the ineffable holiness, the incarnate purity,
lovingly accepts the tender effusion of the sinner. Jesus, the same who

in holy wrath cast out the moneychangers from the temple, the same who implacably unmasked the hypocrisy of the Pharisees, allows the repentant sinner to minister to him and to kiss his feet. And he dismisses her, restored to purity and filled with life, with the words, "Thy faith has saved thee; go in peace."

In the words, "because she has loved much," the role and dignity of the heart is gloriously disclosed by the God-Man. For indeed all the manifestations of Mary Magdalene's loving contrition and repentant love were effusions of her heart. But the words of our Lord and his meekness, his clemency, his mercy toward Mary Magdalene, allow us a glance into the mystery of his Sacred Heart and its ineffable holiness: *Cor Jesu, fons vitae et sanctitatis, miserere nobis*, "Heart of Jesus, source of life and holiness, have mercy on us."

> But Jesus went to the Mount of Olives. And at daybreak he came again into the temple, and all the people came to him; and sitting down he began to teach them.
>
> Now the Scribes and Pharisees brought a woman caught in adultery, and setting her in the midst, said to him, "Master, this woman has just now been caught in adultery. And in the Law Moses commanded us to stone such persons. What, therefore, dost thou say?" Now they were saying this to test him, in order that they might be able to accuse him. But Jesus, stooping down, began to write with his finger on the ground.
>
> But when they continued asking him, he raised himself and said to them, "Let him who is without sin among you be the first to cast a stone at her." And again stooping down, he began to write on the ground. But hearing this, they went away, one by one, beginning with the eldest. And Jesus remained alone, with the woman standing in the midst.
>
> And Jesus, raising himself, said to her, "Woman, where are they? Has no one condemned thee?" She said, "No one, Lord." Then Jesus said, "Neither will I condemn thee. Go thy way, and from now on sin no more" (Jn 8:1–11).

Again the divine mercy radiates into our minds, and our hearts are touched by the breath of the unfathomable mystery of mercy which we found in the attitude of Jesus toward Mary Magdalene. But here it reaches a new dimension. Mary Magdalene approached the Lord full of contrition and adoring love. She washed his feet with her tears and dried them with her hair. The adulterous woman, on the contrary, has been brought to Christ by force. She stands in front of Christ, humiliated, in all her weakness. The Gospel mentions nothing about her contrition; the mercy of Jesus precedes it. The heart of the adulterous woman, face to face with the infinite purity and awe-inspiring holiness of Jesus, is melted by his mercy. A new life is engendered in her soul.

The most extraordinary confrontation of the sinner with Christ is displayed. Christ does not address her immediately; instead he first disarms her pharisaic judges, "Let him who is without sin among you be the first to cast a stone at her."

These words resound through the centuries and aeons, until the end of the world, awakening our consciences when we are tempted to judge our neighbor. Jesus remains silent while those who would judge her leave one by one. But in this silent confrontation, there is a world of mercy, meekness, and charity. It is the mystery of man's iniquity and of God's infinite holiness, the drama of an encounter of man's contrition and God's antecedent mercy. Christ does not so much as look at her directly. He writes in the sand. The confrontation as such suffices to melt the heart of the humiliated and ashamed sinner. By not addressing her immediately, by not even looking at her directly, Christ gives her time, and allows the process of "conversion" to take place without increasing her humiliation. The first word addressed to her after this holy silence is a question, "Has no one condemned thee?" This question again manifests the inexhaustible, tender indulgence of Jesus. The merciful pardoning of the Lord, the eternal judge, the one who alone can condemn or forgive remains hidden in the question. The question of condemnation is only indirectly touched upon in his asking her whether those who have no more than a juridical right to condemn her have done so. And when she answers, "No one, Lord," Jesus says, "Neither will I condemn thee." The pardon itself is bestowed with a holy discretion. Only at the end does he turn directly to her with an exhortation directed toward the future, the blissful words, "Go thy way, and from now on sin no more," referring to the new life of the converted sinner, of the resurrected soul.

Indeed, in the face of this overwhelming mercy, this tender indulgence, this divine patience dwelling in the Heart of Jesus, we fall on our knees and pray: *Cor Jesu, patiens et multae misericordiae, miserere nobis*, "Heart of Jesus, patient and abounding in mercy, have mercy on us."

> Then Peter came up to him and said, "Lord, how often shall
> my brother sin against me, and I forgive him? Up to seven
> times?" Jesus said to him, "I do not say to thee seven times,
> but seventy times seven" (Mt 18:21–22).

These words again lift us into the "new world" of Christ. The spirit of forgiveness is presented to us in an unlimitedness so thoroughly opposed to the tendencies of our fallen nature.

Forgiveness has a great affinity to mercy, yet it is clearly different from it. Mercy in its literal meaning is primarily a divine virtue. Man's mercifulness is only an analogy to the divine mercy. Christ the Son of God is merciful in the primary authentic sense, in which we can never be merciful. In him, mercy and pardon converge. His pardoning of Mary Magdalene and of the adulterous woman are typical flowerings of divine mercy.

Yet divine forgiving and human forgiveness differ still more than divine mercy and human mercifulness. Divine pardoning refers to sin, that is, to intrinsic moral evil; human forgiving refers only to the objective evil inflicted upon us. In forgiving a wrong done to us, we overcome all bitterness toward the person who offended us; we turn lovingly toward him. But we do clearly realize that our forgiving in no way refers to the moral evil implied in harming us. The objective disharmony created by sin cannot be dissolved by our forgiving. This is possible only through God's pardoning. Thus we hear the Pharisees ask, Who is this man who forgives sins?

While forgiving and mercifulness have a great affinity, they are still two different attitudes in man, whereas divine pardon and divine mercy are interwoven in Christ.

In mercy we renounce a "right" which we have toward another person. The unmerciful servant, for example, does not want to renounce a claim he has on another servant. Forgiveness, on the contrary, refers to a wrong done to us. The opposite of forgiving is revenge; the opposite of mercifulness is an insistence on our claim or title. Shylock refuses to be merciful. In the case of mercifulness, we remit a person's debt, we lovingly release him from an obligation. Again it is mercy which moves a person to refrain from punishing a guilty person, though he has authority to do so. Mercy also prompts a man in a morally stronger position not to use his advantage against another.

Forgiveness, on the contrary, is concerned with our inner stance toward the offender. Any grudge, revengeful tendency, bitterness, enmity, feud is dissolved in forgiving. We cancel the "account" in our soul on which his wrong against us may have been carefully recorded.

Thus we see that, though deeply related to mercy, forgiveness is a new differentiation, another manifestation of the one infinite flow which is the very core of all supernatural morality, namely charity.

Again we witness the contrast between man and the God-Man, Christ. Christ's commandment to forgive is reverently and lovingly accepted by Peter. In his ardor and readiness to follow the Master, in his desire to know precisely how to follow this commandment, he says, "Lord, how often shall my brother sin against me, and I forgive him? Up to seven times?"

In spite of all his readiness, of all his desire to follow Christ's commandments, of his devotion to Christ, his question still reflects a human limitation. It is Peter before Pentecost. And against the background of this spirit of forgiveness, which is still conditional, limited, restricted, the answer of Christ is resplendent, "I do not say to thee seven times, but seventy times seven." Again we see how the fire which Christ has come to bring to earth destroys all barriers and all limitations. Again we witness the irruption of divine superabundance into the limitedness of the world. It is the breath of the Holy Spirit. And again the glory of the Sacred Humanity of Christ displays itself before our minds. "Not seven, but seventy times seven" are words of the Redeemer, redeeming words, filled with the flow of the infinite charity. It is the voice of the Sacred Heart: *Cor Jesu, tabernaculum Altissimi, miserere nobis*, "Heart of Jesus, tabernacle of the Most High, have mercy on us."

> Then the mother of the sons of Zebedee came to him with her sons; and worshipping, she made a request of him. He said to her, "What dost thou want?" She said to him, "Command that these my two sons may sit, one at thy right hand and one at thy left hand, in thy kingdom." But Jesus answered and said, "You do not know what you are asking for. Can you drink of the cup of which I am about to drink?" They said to him, "We can." He said to them, "Of my cup you shall indeed drink; but as for sitting at my right hand and at my left, that is not mine to give you, but it belongs to those for whom it has been prepared by my Father" (Mt:20 20–23).

The petition of the mother of John and James makes plain that her love was intermingled with ambition for her sons. We see the effusion of a heart tainted with a naive egoism. But Jesus does not rebuke her, nor does he chide her. He only answers in an unheard-of clemency, "You do not know what you are asking for." Even the apostles John and James show a naive projection of earthly categories and standards into the Kingdom of God. Without realizing the full meaning of the "chalice," and in a mixture of devotion and touching readiness, on the one hand, with ambition and self-assurance, on the other, they join in their mother's petition.

Again Jesus does not chide them. He only lays bare the inadequacy of their petition. The petition of the mother and of her two sons evokes the anger of the other apostles. It is understandable that it scandalized them. But in their anger there is also an element of ambition. They are not scandalized on account of the inadequacy of the petition, but because of the presumptuousness of the sons of Zebedee, and especially of their mother, to claim a favor for them. Their very protest reveals that they too have not yet completely overcome the standards of earthly glory.

But again, instead of rebuking their anger, instead of humiliating them, Jesus expounds the new rule of supernatural glory and the true grandeur of humility to them. Indeed this divine clemency of Jesus, this meekness toward his disciples, allows us another glimpse at the holy affectivity dwelling in the Sacred Heart of Jesus. We fall on our knees and adore him: *Cor Jesu, domus Dei et porta caeli, miserere nobis*, "Heart of Jesus, house of God, and gate of Heaven, have mercy on us."

> But he spoke this parable also to some who trusted in themselves as being just and despised others. "Two men went up to the temple to pray, the one a Pharisee and the other a publican. The Pharisee stood and began to pray thus within himself, 'O God, I thank thee that I am not like the rest of men, robbers, dishonest, adulterers, or even like this publican. I fast twice a week; I pay tithes of all that I possess.' But the publican, standing afar off, would not so much as lift up his eyes to heaven, but kept striking his breast, saying, 'O God, be merciful to me the sinner!'
>
> I tell you, this man went back to his home justified rather than the other; for everyone who exalts himself shall be hum-

bled, and he who humbles himself shall be exalted"
(Lk 18:9–14).

This parable sheds a divine light upon our minds. A new morality
is disclosed. In this parable, Christ reveals the mystery of humility in
all its victorious beauty. The sinner who humbles himself goes home
justified; the proud "just" man who exalts himself returns from the
temple unjustified. Without humility, all his punctiliousness and conformity does not profit the Pharisee, but the power of humility and its
value is such that by itself it suffices to justify the sinner. Again this
parable bears the unmistakable seal of the world above. All natural
standards fade away before the eternal words, "everyone who exalts
himself shall be humbled, and he who humbles himself shall be exalted."

These words of Jesus are the breath of redeeming holiness; they
embody the irruption of divine light into this world. Indeed, upon
hearing these words of Christ, it is not only *phase Domini,* the "passover
of the Lord," but the infusion of his sacred truth into this world. He
who is not shaken by the mystery of humility, who does not understand
that the world became a new one, a different one, after this parable was
taught by Christ, does not really grasp the *lumen Christi,* "the light of
Christ." He who fails to realize the spiritual revolution which is
implied in these words—a revolution from above resulting from divine
revelation—has not understood the divine message, the *euangelion.*
The man whose soul is not pierced by these words as by a sword,
whose view of the world and of himself has not been overturned, has
not understood this parable.

And in this parable which reveals the length and height and depth
of humility to us, we are drawn under the spell of the Sacred Heart of
Jesus. Being immersed by Jesus in the mystery of humility, we are also
deigned to see a ray of the infinite holiness which dwells in the Sacred
Heart of the God-Man who said, *Discite a me, quia sum mitis et humilis
corde,* "Learn of me, for I am meek and humble of heart."

> But he also spoke a parable to those invited, observing how
> they were choosing the first places at table, and he said to
> them, "When thou art invited to a wedding feast, do not
> recline in the first place, lest perhaps one more distinguished
> than thou have been invited by him, and he who invited thee
> and him come and say to thee, 'Make room for this man'; and

then thou begin with shame to take the last place. But when thou art invited, go and recline in the last place; that when he who invited thee comes in, he may say to thee, 'Friend, go up higher!' Then thou wilt be honored in the presence of all who are at table with thee. For everyone who exalts himself shall be humbled, and he who humbles himself shall be exalted" (Lk 14:7–11).

The theme of this parable is again the glorious mystery of humility. It is not the modesty of the one who does not think highly of himself and thus remains in the background in an attitude of resignation. Attractive as it may be, modesty is a mere natural virtue. We find modest men even among pagans. Modesty is the result of a wholesome objectivity about oneself which enables a person to realize his own limits and the superiority of others. The modest man certainly deserves praise, but it is not to the modest man that Christ promises exaltation; it is to the one who possesses humility, a specific feature of the new creature in Christ. It is this glorious virtue which moves the guest to take the last seat.

This parable discloses the mysterious aspect of humility that implies the gesture of placing oneself below the level on which we naturally stand. It is the humility of a Saint Francis which induces him to become a beggar. It is the dimension of humility which implies a faint analogy to the mysterious condescension of the God-Man himself, to his divine humility. We hear the blissful words, the loving exaltation of the Lord, *Amice, ascende superius*, "Friend, go higher," in which the mercy of God and his love for humility are revealed. Indeed, the same words, *qui se exaltat humiliabitur*, "he who exalts himself shall be humbled," which lay bare the fundamental importance of humility, assume here a new content by making apparent a new dimension of its nature.

Again, we are carried into the *regnum sanctitatis et gratiae*, "the kingdom of sanctity and grace," and we breathe the atmosphere of redemption. In grasping the new dimension of humility, which is a reflection of the mystery of divine humility in Jesus, we approach more and more the holy wealth dwelling in the Sacred Heart of Jesus. *Cor Jesu, salus in te sperantium, miserere nobis*, "Heart of Jesus, salvation of all who trust in thee, have mercy on us."

But Jesus called them to him, and said, "You know that the rulers of the Gentiles lord it over them, and their great men

exercise authority over them. Not so is it among you. On the
contrary, whoever wishes to become great among you shall be
your servant; and whoever wishes to be first among you shall
be your slave; even as the Son of Man has not come to be
served but to serve, and to give his life as a ransom for many"
(Mt 20:25–28).

These words overturn all natural categories of glory, fame, and
lordship. Whereas the words, "He who humbles himself shall be exalted," apply to every human person, the words, "whoever wishes to be
first among you shall be your slave," apply to him who is to be first. Yet
serving is not a means for attaining the position of lordship found
among the Gentiles; it is a completely new conception of lordship of
which serving is the very soul. The one called by God to lead, to command, to be first, should above all serve others. This is the law of the
New Testament. In it the antithesis between the "world" with its laws
and the kingdom of heaven is clearly revealed. It is the abyss between
the two cities of St. Augustine. But this law of the New Testament is
not only the antithesis to the world in the sense of the Holy Scriptures,
it also overthrows all valid yet merely natural categories by gloriously
surpassing them. We feel the mysteriously liberating breath of the
supernatural while listening to these words.

Yet when Christ says, "Even as the Son of Man has not come to be
served but to serve," (*filius hominis non venit ministrari sed ministrare*),
we are confronted not only with the Law of the New Testament, but
with the very mystery of the Incarnation. It is the God-Man, Christ,
the same Lord who said, *Mihi est data omnis potestas in caelo et in terra*,
"All power in heaven and earth has been given to me," who pro-
nounces these words. The mystery of divine charity and the mystery
of divine humility illuminate our minds. To serve is an outflow of charity as well as of humility. In the words: "Even as the Son of Man
has . . . come . . . to give his life as a ransom for many," divine charity
and divine humility reach their ultimate expression as embodied in the
mystery of redemption. And at the same time that Christ speaks of
himself, we are granted a more direct glance into his Sacred Heart.

The unfathomable charity and divine humility dwelling in his
Sacred Heart moves our hearts, and we fall on our knees adoring him:
Cor Jesu, in quo Pater sibi bene complacuit, miserere nobis, "Heart of Jesus,
in which the Father was well pleased, have mercy on us."

"And further I say to you, it is easier for a camel to pass through an eye of a needle, than for a rich man to enter the kingdom of heaven" (Mt 19:24).

"Amen I say to you, the publicans and harlots are entering the kingdom of God before you" (Mt 21:31).

"So if thy right eye is an occasion of sin to thee, pluck it out and cast it from thee" (Mt 5:29).

"But I say to you not to resist the evildoer; on the contrary, if someone strike thee on the right cheek, turn to him the other also" (Mt 5:39).

"Do not think that I come to send peace upon the earth; I have come to bring a sword, not peace. For I have come to set a man at variance with his father, and a daughter with her mother, and a daughter-in-law with her mother-in-law" (Mt 10:34–36).

The terrifying emphasis in these words is a reflection of a divine unlimitedness. It would be a radical misunderstanding of these words of Christ to see in them a mere expression of a natural emphasis which is to be found in a passionate rebuke. This emphasis of a natural kind always has the character of a passing momentary emotion. But the terrifying severity and absoluteness in these words of Christ are neither the result of a momentary emotion nor have they anything in common in quality or nature with this merely natural excessiveness.

But what matters especially here is to grasp the contrast between the divine unlimitedness and that natural excessiveness worshipped by the Promethean type of man who attempts to surpass the limits of his creaturehood. We often find this ethos in literature and in life. Those Promethean types include in their aversion to all limitation a scorn for the great value of true measure. They see in every measure an element of pharisaism; they are in love with boundlessness for its own sake. They praise a heroic moral act not because of its goodness, but because of its heroic character.

On the contrary, the boundlessness with which we are confronted in these words of Christ does not oppose the true value of measure. It contains *per eminentiam* all the values of true measure while surpassing them infinitely. In distinction to natural boundlessness, it is not nourished by the fire proper to a Dionysian dynamism or a Promethean excessivity. It is not an over-dimensioned natural affectivity. This natural boundlessness, moreover, is a merely apparent boundlessness which consists in a dynamism escaping any measure; in its immeasurable overflowing it has something indefinite. This indefinite dynamism is in reality typically limited; it is an attempt to attain boundlessness by mere quantity.

The divine boundless affectivity in the words of Christ, on the contrary, is neither merely dynamic nor indefinite. The ultimate seriousness of sin, of the offense to God, of man's vocation, of man's sanctification, come here to the fore in their true dimension, it is the unlimited import of obedience to God, of the glorification of God, of the redemption offered to us by Christ.

The ethos contained in these words is boundless because these things of God are unlimited. It is part of the infinitude of God, of his infinite love, his infinite mercy, his infinite holiness. Natural dimensions are infinitely surpassed by the irruption of the divine fire. This heroic superabundance which we find in the lives of the saints is possible only through Christ—*per ipsum, cum ipso et in ipso*, "through him, with him, and in him." Every attempt to attain unlimitedness on the natural level—that is to say, by our own nature—is doomed to failure.

The unlimitedness of the affectivity of Christ, which is a scandal for the worshipper of measure, is, for our purely natural approach, a sword dividing soul and spirit. But precisely this very fact reveals the glorious superabundance which vanquishes all natural categories and inebriates our souls with the breath of infinity.

All this inebriating unlimitedness, this boundlessness, is interwoven with holy sobriety. It is the *ebrietas* of which the Liturgy sings, *Laeti bibamus sobriam ebrietatem Spiritus sancti*, "joyfully we drink the sober intoxication of the Holy Spirit."

This superabundant affectivity of Christ, his boundless charity, his unlimited humility, his inexhaustible mercy, his glorious divine majesty, all reveal the pulsation of the Sacred Heart of Jesus: *Cor Jesu, virtutum, omnium abyssus, miserere nob is*, "Heart of Jesus, abyss of all virtues, have mercy on us."

CHAPTER TWO
The Mystery of the Sacred Heart

Immersing ourselves in many passages of the Gospel, we tried to discover the wealth of the Sacred Heart of Jesus and to catch a glimpse of the quality of his Sacred Heart and its holy affectivity. Now we want to delve into those passages of the Gospel in which our Lord directly discloses the life of his Sacred Heart, those sublime passages which grant us an insight into this most intimate holy secret. We are granted a glimpse of the wounds inflicted on his Heart by the infidelity of his disciples, by the insipidity of Jerusalem and of the chosen people. We are privileged to divine his tender love for his disciples, his underlying outlook at his supreme sacrifice, his anxieties, his loneliness.

We are even granted a glance into a secret of his Sacred Heart incomparably more sublime, namely the motions directed to his heavenly Father, his abandonment to God, his supreme sacrifice, his infinite love. In these intimate revelations of his Heart, Christ's human nature certainly manifests itself in a specific fashion. And yet we are confronted with the great mystery that it is precisely in these manifestations of his Sacred Humanity that his divinity is revealed in a most intimate way. It is the mystery that his Heart is substantially united to the Second Person of the Holy Trinity.

Moreover, in the last chapter, we tried to divine the holy affectivity dwelling in the Heart of Jesus. In focusing on the epiphany of God in the Sacred Humanity of Christ, we tried to delve more and more into the mystery of the Sacred Heart. Now, concentrating on those passages in which Jesus grants us an insight into the life of his Sacred Heart, it is above all the reality of his truly human nature which is disclosed. It is the reality of *et homo factus est*, "and he became man." Yet, simultaneously all these effusions of his Sacred Heart are filled with the holiness which makes it an epiphany of God.

The ineffable qualitative sublimity of these effusions of his Sacred Heart and their truly human character testify to the mystery of the Incarnation. And it is the mysterious tension proper to the Incarnation that gives to each of these passages of the Gospel a unique, dramatic character.

Indeed, when the Lord reveals the secret of his Heart, its vulnerability, its unprotectedness, its human love, we cannot but adore him. For all the specifically human features are but a fruit, a result, an expression of his infinite divine love and condescending divine humility.

Thus the more his humanity is stressed (always in the context of the sacred, ineffably holy humanity), the more adorable is the mystery of divine infinite love.

It is especially in these moments in which the mystery of the Incarnation is most resplendent that we are forced to fall on our knees and to adore him with the apostle St. Thomas: *Domine meus, et Deus meus*, "My Lord and my God."

> The Son of Man is to be betrayed into the hands of men,
> and they will kill him; and on the third day he will rise again.
> And they were exceedingly sorry (Mt 17:21).

In all the predictions of the passion, there is a resonance of deep sorrow: Jesus discloses his vulnerable, loving heart. It is true that every time the passion is predicted, the glorious resurrection is also mentioned. And yet at the moment of the prediction, a sublime sorrow and a tragic note prevail. For before the glory of the resurrection stands the unfathomable suffering of Gethsemane and the death on the cross, and the ring of the voice of his Heart betrays this dominance.

In the surprisingly strong rebuke of St. Peter after the first prediction, we see this tragic note. "And Peter taking him aside, began to chide him, saying, 'Far be it from thee, O Lord; this will never happen to thee.' He turned and said to Peter, 'Get behind me, satan, thou art a scandal to me; for thou dost not mind the things of God, but those of men'" (Mt 16:22–23).

The words of St. Peter were words of love filled with the conviction and the hope that this prediction would never come true. Yet behind his chiding of the Lord, there was also the desire to avoid giving scandal. Peter's words made it clear that he had not yet understood the mystery of redemption. And the emphatic rebuke of the Lord indicates that in this moment the theme is above all the impending passion, and so we hear the voice of the unprotected heart of Jesus which offers itself to God for the redemption of man: *Cor Jesu, propitiatio pro peccatis nostris, miserere nobis*, "Heart of Jesus, atonement for our iniquities, have mercy on us."

> And when he drew near and saw the city, he wept over it, saying, "If thou hadst known, in this thy day, even thou, the things that are for thy peace" (Lk 19:41).

Again Jesus discloses his Heart in weeping over Jerusalem. Tears, and especially tears of sorrow, are an effusion of the heart and a specially intimate one. Tears of the Son of Man must move us thus to our very marrow. The same person of whom the Credo sings, *Deum de Deo, lumen de lumine, Deum verum de Deo vero*, "God from God, light from light, true God from true God," sheds tears! The mystery of the Incarnation, of the substantial union of the human nature with the Word, is present in these holy tears, in this personal, intimate effusion of the Heart of Jesus. *Cor Jesu, omni laude dignissimum, miserere nobis*, "Heart of Jesus, most worthy of all praise, have mercy on us."

But Jesus grants us an incomparably more intimate insight into his Sacred Heart in the raising of Lazarus.

> The sisters therefore sent to him, saying, "Lord, behold, he whom thou lovest is sick." But when Jesus heard this, he said to them, "This sickness is not unto death, but for the glory of God, that through it the Son of God may be glorified." Now Jesus loved Martha and her sister Mary, and Lazarus (Jn 11:3–5).

Already the words, "whom thou lovest is sick," and, "now Jesus loved Martha and her sister Mary and Lazarus," are a unique disclosure of the Sacred Heart. These words, "now Jesus loved," do not refer to the charity with which Jesus embraces every man, but to a special love for Lazarus and his sisters. Certainly even in the divine charity there are differences of degree. It is not that God loves everyone equally, though he loves everyone infinitely. God loves the Holy Virgin more than any other saint. But here, the love of Jesus for Lazarus, Martha, and Mary is not only distinguished by degree from the charity with which he turns to every sinner; there is a note of special personal tenderness in this love, an intimate effusion of his Heart. St. John thus informs us about something intimate and personal, something which is not included in the disclosure of Christ's infinite charity. Otherwise, St. John would not mention it expressly as a characteristic of the relation of Jesus to them. It is a remark similar to the one concerning St. John himself when John is called "the disciple whom the Lord loved."

It is only with a trembling heart and with the utmost reverence that we receive this message, and that we are informed of this human, personal, intimate motion of the Sacred Heart in which there dwells all the plenitude of the divinity. We can grasp or divine the sublimity and unfathomable preciousness of this human love of Jesus only if we constantly keep in mind that it is the Son of God, the Word, to whom this human nature is substantially united. Against this background only can the overwhelming sweetness and intimate splendor of this human love living in the Sacred Heart reveal itself: *Cor Jesu, rex et centrum omnium cordium, miserere nobis*, "Heart of Jesus, king and center of all hearts, have mercy on us."

But the Gospel narrating the raising of Lazarus grants us a still deeper insight into the personal, secret motion of the Sacred Heart:

> When, therefore, Mary came where Jesus was, and saw him, she fell at his feet, and said to him, "Lord if thou hadst been here, my brother would not have died." When, therefore, Jesus saw her weeping, and the Jews who had come with her weeping, he groaned in spirit and was troubled, and said, "Where have you laid him?" They said to him, "Lord, come and see." And Jesus wept. The Jews therefore said, "See how he loved him" (Jn 11:32–36).

Jesus groaned in his spirit and was troubled upon seeing Mary weep, in witnessing her sorrow at the terrible reality of death. He who knew that he would raise Lazarus, and restore him to his sisters, "groaned in spirit and was troubled."

The plenitude of his Heart, the full response to the human aspect of death, the tender personal love for Mary and for Lazarus, reveal the full humanity of Christ, his being made equal to man in everything except sin.

And Jesus wept. These tears are an effusion of his Sacred Heart still more intimate than the tears shed over Jerusalem's fate. They are the expression of a more intimate, more personal love.

Indeed in the raising of Lazarus, the Heart of the God-Man is bared before us in a mysterious way. First we witness the expression of his human love for Mary, Martha, and Lazarus, of his sorrow, of his compassion with their sorrow, of the full experience of the human aspect of death and all its horror. Then we hear the words of Jesus revealing his Sacred Heart in gratitude to his heavenly Father, "Father, I give thee thanks that thou has heard me. Yet I knew that thou always hearest me" (Jn 11:41–42).

And by raising Lazarus, the divinity of Christ again is over-whelmingly revealed.

Inconceivable mystery of the Incarnation and ineffable sublimity and holiness of the Sacred Heart of the God-Man! The same who by his word restores Lazarus to life "groaned in his spirit" and wept to see Mary weep. Fathomless holiness of this Heart, most intimate core of his Sacred Humanity, in its human plenitude and vulnerability and yet substantially united to the Word! Deep expression of the mystery of the Incarnation, of the tension between human and divine in Christ! Simultaneously in the quality of his Humanity, in its transfigured holiness, it is an epiphany of God. *Cor Jesu in quo habitat omnis plenitudo divinitatis, miserere nobis*, "Heart of Jesus, wherein abides the fullness of the Godhead, have mercy on us."

> Mary therefore took a pound of ointment, genuine nard of great value, and anointed the feet of Jesus, and with her hair wiped his feet dry. And the house was filled with the odor of the ointment. Then one of his disciples, Judas Iscariot, he who was about to betray him, said, "Why was this ointment not sold for three hundred denarii, and given to the poor?" Now he said this not that he cared for the poor, but because he was a thief, and holding the purse, used to take what was put into it. Jesus therefore said, "Let her be—that she may keep it for the day of my burial. For the poor you have always with you, but you do not always have me" (Jn 12:3–8).

In the words, "For the poor you have always with you, but you do not always have me," we hear the ring of a love filled with sorrow. Here we are not focused on the fundamental importance of these words, hinting at the primacy of the love of Christ over the love of neighbor. We are now listening to the voice of the Heart of Jesus which can be heard in these words. They contain a personal note, an unveiling of his

Heart. It is the Sacred Heart, unprotected, exposed to all the emnity and hatred of the world. It is the Sacred Heart in all its unlimited capacity for suffering, in its infinite love. In these words we find the love for his disciples and sorrow over the impending departure. "For in pouring this ointment on my body, she has done it for my burial."

The note of sorrow found in the predictions of the passion is increased here. And the more we approach the passion and death of our Lord, the more the Sacred Heart is unveiled, and the more we are exposed to the radiations of the Heart of Jesus. *Cor Jesu, templum Dei sanctum, miserere nobis*, "Heart of Jesus, holy temple of God, have mercy on us."

> And he said to them, "I have greatly desired to eat this passover with you before I suffer; for I say to you that I will eat of it no more, until it has been fulfilled in the kingdom of God" (Lk 22:14–16).

In general the Lord addressed his disciples in revealing divine truth which they were called to transmit to the world. He speaks to them in parables, gives them admonitions and commandments. He gives them the power of binding and loosing; he institutes them as his apostles.

Certainly on many occasions, the love for his disciples finds an indirect expression, yet these words are a unique manifestation of his Sacred Heart, in them there lives a tender, personal love intermingled with the sorrow over his impending departure.

The same Christ who, when speaking of himself does so mostly in terms of his mission, now in this solemn moment reveals something which takes place in his Sacred Heart, a personal desire, fruit of the tender love for his disciples dwelling in his Heart. *Cor Jesu, de cujus plenitudine omnes nos accepimus, miserere nobis*, "Heart of Jesus, of whose fullness we have all received, have mercy on us."

> Now when evening arrived, he reclined at table with the twelve disciples. And while they were eating, he said, "Amen I say to you, one of you will betray me." And being very much saddened they began each to say, "Is it I, Lord?" But he answered and said, "He who dips his hand with me in the dish, he will betray me. The Son of Man indeed goes his way, as it is written of him; but woe to that man by whom the Son of Man

is betrayed! It were better for that man if he had not been born." And Judas who betrayed him answered and said, "Is it I, Rabbi?" He said to him, "Thou hast said it" (Mt 26:20–25).

We hear the voice of the Heart of Jesus in the words, "Amen I say to you, one of you will betray me." They transmit his sorrow over the offense to God; the sorrow for Judas Iscariot whom he loved; the wounding of his heart through the ingratitude, the infidelity, the hostility of Judas whom he had chosen as one of his apostles. And this very expression of his "being wounded" is a manifestation of his Sacred Heart, of this great and personal secret of the God-Man.

The wounded Heart of Jesus is still more revealed in the prediction of Peter's denial, "You will all be scandalized this night because of me. . . . But Peter answered and said to him, 'Even though all shall be scandalized because of thee, I will never be scandalized'" (Mt 26:31–32).

Against the background of Peter's ardent love and fidelity, of his bold assurance that nothing could sever him from Christ, the answer of the Lord discloses the deep suffering, the exposure of his unprotected Heart to the infidelity, to the lack of perseverance, to the wavering frailty of even the most loving, most faithful and devoted apostle. "Amen, I say to thee, this very night, before a cock crows, thou wilt deny me three times" (Mt 26:34).

It is as if step by step a deeper stratum of the Heart of the God-Man is revealed to us: first the wound inflicted by the betrayal of Judas; then the wound inflicted by the denial of the prince of the apostles, the very one to whom Jesus had said, "Thou art Peter and upon this rock I will build my church."

Certainly in itself, Judas' betrayal was an incomparably greater offense to God than the denial of Peter; it was also an incomparably greater evil for Judas than the denial was for Peter. Thus the words of Christ, "It would have been better had this man not been born." But the wound inflicted on the Sacred Heart of Jesus by the denial of the one whom he had chosen as the prince of the apostles and who loved him so ardently, was a still more personal, more intimate one.

We are confronted with the two aspects of the *mysterium iniquitatis*, "the mystery of sin"—the apostasy of the wicked and the failure of the one who loves God, who is sure that he will never be unfaithful.

The sublime quality of the sorrow of Jesus revealed here differs radically from any suffering of even the most noble human being. It is the heart of the Son of Man whose voice we hear and also the voice of the heart of the God-Man. *Cor Jesu, saturatum opprobriis, miserere nobis,* "Heart of Jesus, glutted with reproaches, have mercy on us."

Again a new dimension of the Heart of Jesus is revealed to us in Gethsemane, "And he took with him Peter and the two sons of Zebedee, and he began to be saddened and exceedingly troubled. Then he said to them, 'My soul is sad, even unto death. Wait here and watch with me.' And going forward a little, he fell prostrate and prayed, saying, 'Father, if it is possible, let this cup pass away from me; yet not as I will, but as thou willest'" (Mt 26:37–39).

In the words, "My soul is sad, even unto death," there is no longer only the ring of a voice trembling with deep sorrow; there is no longer only a fact mentioned by Jesus, which reveals implicitly the wound of his Heart; instead there is the direct revelation of his Heart. Jesus speaks of himself and of the state of his soul. He lifts the veil from the personal, intimate secret of his Heart.

We are confronted with the *coincidentia oppositorum*, "the joining of opposites," embodied in the mystery of the Incarnation. On the one hand, the sadness unto death is a fundamental manifestation of the human nature of Christ; it reveals to us Jesus as Son of Man. On the other hand, the quality of this sadness, its mysterious sublimity, its expiating power, its intimate connection with the infinite divine love of Christ, is part of the epiphany of God in the Sacred Humanity of Christ. Again the character of unlimited suffering of Jesus in Gethsemane is possible only in the God-Man. For this suffering contains the sea of noble tears shed by all men who have ever lived or will live until the end of the world; it reflects all the disharmony brought about by the fall of man. The dimension of this suffering surpasses all human categories, though suffering itself is possible only for a human being.

Yet, if in the words, "My soul is sad, even unto death," Jesus unveils his Heart in the most direct way, he grants us a still more intimate revelation of his Sacred Heart in the words, "Father, all things are possible to Thee. Remove this cup from me" (Mk 14:36). It is the deepest, most secret chord of his Heart, the voice of his Heart calling to God the Father.

Yet, only in the light of the ultimate abandonment to God embodied in the final words, "yet not what I will, but what thou willest," does the foregoing petition assume its full impact; and only through the earlier petition does the final word assume its full, genuine reality, and its glorious truth. The very sequence of these two words grants us an overwhelming revelation of the Sacred Heart. *Cor Jesu, attritum propter scelera nostra, miserere nobis*, "Heart of Jesus, bruised for our sins, have mercy on us."

Unlike all the teachings of our Lord, unlike the revelation of his mission, the theme of the words on the cross is neither revelation of divine truth nor self-revelation. Nor are these words an explicit unveiling of the heart of Jesus, such as the words *Desiderio desideravi manducare hoc pascha vobiscum*, "With desire I have desired to eat this meal with you." The theme here is the redeeming passion, so that many of the words of Christ are directed to his heavenly Father. We are allowed to witness this most sublime mysterious event, this most intimate divine action in which the redeeming passion alone is the theme. Yet it is precisely here that the mystery of suffering, destitution, and obedience unto death reveals, in a certain way, more of his Sacred Heart than any word in which Christ addressed himself explicitly to mankind. It is in the moment in which the redeeming action is the exclusive theme that in one sense the most intimate unveiling of the Sacred Heart is granted to us.

In the veneration of the Sacred Heart of Jesus, our Lord's passion plays a central role. There is, indeed, a deep and essential relation between the heart and the capacity to suffer, and the entire passion is an unveiling of the secrets of the Sacred Heart.

"Father, forgive them, for they do not know what they are doing" (Lk 23:34). In this supreme moment, Christ speaks as the Son of Man, in contrast to all the situations in which, speaking as the Son of God, he pardons sinners himself.

Yet in asking God to pardon his enemies, Christ implicitly forgives them the injury done to him. This is a human forgiving, the same forgiveness which Christ commands us to have. But above all, we are confronted with his ultimate, merciful charity; Christ not only asks God to pardon his murderers, he even excuses them on account of their ignorance. The Son of Man places, as it were, his protecting arms before his murderers.

We are deigned to witness in the Sacred Heart the glory of merciful charity and sublime forgiveness. *Cor Jesu, fons totius consolationis, miserere nobis*, "Heart of Jesus, source of all consolation, have mercy on us."

"Amen I say to thee, this day thou shalt be with me in paradise" (Lk 23:43).

In these words Jesus speaks primarily as God, as the one who can pardon sin and promise paradise to the good thief. But here too the voice of his Sacred Heart can be heard. There is a ring of holy joy in these words. The overwhelming response given to this one appeal of the converted thief is not only a pardoning, but the assurance of immediate beatitude. In this respect it surpasses the words spoken to Mary Magdalene or to the adulteress. Certainly they are spoken to a man on a cross, a man facing immediate death, whereas Mary Magdalene and the adulterous woman still had a life to live, and they might still go astray.

Nevertheless our Lord's superabundant response to the good thief is not only a manifestation of the boundless mercy of God, it reveals also a joy in the Heart of Jesus over the man who recognizes the divinity of the crucified Lord at the very moment in which the apostles believe that all their hope is buried. *Cor Jesu, dives in omnes qui invocant te, miserere nobis*, "Heart of Jesus, rich unto all that call upon thee, have mercy on us."

> Now there were standing by the cross of Jesus his mother and his mother's sister, Mary of Cleophas, and Mary Magdalene. When Jesus, therefore, saw his mother and the disciple standing by, whom he loved, he said to his mother, "Woman, behold thy son." Then he said to the disciple, "Behold thy mother." And from that hour the disciple took her into his home (Jn 19:25–27).

Here again Christ speaks primarily as the Son of Man and not as Lord and Redeemer. These words embody an utterance of his Heart, of his love for the holy Virgin and for St. John, and of his sorrow in leaving them. He confides his Mother to John. Certainly, these words also imply the solemn institution of the Holy Virgin as the Mother of all men, and as such they are spoken out of the holy authority of the Redeemer and Son of God.

The character of a sublime last will of the Son of Man, the breath of love for his holy Mother and St. John, give to these words a specific intimacy. *Cor Jesu, in sinu Virginis Matris a Spiritu Sancto formatum, miserere nobis*, "Heart of Jesus, formed by the Holy Spirit in the womb of the Virgin Mary, have mercy on us."

After this Jesus, knowing that all things were now accomplished, that the Scripture might be fulfilled, said, "I thirst" (Jn 19:28).

Again the theme here is not revelation but the passion. The agony of his Sacred Body finds an expression in a word implying a request directed to men, to his executioners, to give him to drink. If the "*Eli, Eli, lama sabachtani*" is the deepest descent into the unfathomable abyss of suffering, the destitution of the soul, the *Sitio*, "I thirst," is the deepest descent into another dimension, that of human frailty, of man's dependence upon his body. It is an ineffable expression of the divine humility, of the one "who emptied himself taking the nature of a slave."

In this supreme moment we are reaching in the role assumed by the body a culmination of the tension of the mystery of the Incarnation. The Lord who is never recorded as mentioning any bodily distress expresses his "thirst" in this supreme moment. His fatigue is mentioned only by the evangelist in the Gospel of the Samaritan woman, and his hunger in the Gospel of the temptations. But here a descent into human helplessness takes place to the point of calling on the "mercy" of his executioners. Mystery of divine humility! The Lord who always gives, who changes water into wine, who feeds the five thousand with five loaves of bread, who gives sight to the blind, who wakes Lazarus from death, this Lord speaks of his thirst here, in the supreme moment of his sacrifice. In this word, revelation is even less the theme than in any other word spoken from the Cross. The fact that it implies an appeal to man makes it the very antithesis of revelation, a pure expression of his suffering, while yet revealing a deep secret of his passion. Moreover, this implicit request is not addressed to his disciples but to the merciless soldiers. Christ's appeal to their mercy makes this cry the most dramatic expression of his suffering and of his destitution, the deprivation of all his divine might and glory.

And this word *Sitio* resounds through all the history of mankind in its mysterious sublimity, piercing our hearts, awakening us to our guilt, and melting our hearts in love. *Cor Jesu, Verbo Dei substantialiter unitum, miserere nobis*, "Heart of Jesus, united hypostatically to the Word of God, have mercy on us."

Now from the sixth hour there was darkness over the whole land until the ninth hour. But about the ninth hour Jesus cried out with a loud voice, saying, "*Eli, Eli, lama sabacthani,*" that is, "My God, my God, why hast thou forsaken me?" (Mt 27:45–46).

Here the mystery of the Incarnation reaches its most extraordinary manifestation. The one who forgives sins, the Lord who will sit *ad dexteram Patris*, "on the right hand of the Father," speaks as if deprived of his divinity in supreme solitude and destitution. Here the tension of the true God and true man reaches a point in which Christ's human nature seems almost to veil the divine nature. And yet this moment is an ineffable revelation of the mystery of the Incarnation and redemption when seen in the light of the resurrection, and when understood in the continuity of the entire epiphany of God in Christ.

Here Jesus unveils his heart more than ever before. He allows us to witness this ultimate descent into the unfathomable abyss of suffering, this utter destitution of the one of whom the Church sings, *Benedictus qui venit in nomine Domini*, "Blessed is he who comes in the name of the Lord." The suffering that we are allowed to divine here surpasses all human dimensions, and yet it is essentially human. In it all the suffering of mankind is at once contained and vanquished. *Cor Jesu, usque ad mortem obediens factum, miserere nobis*, "Heart of Jesus, made obedient unto death, have mercy on us."

> Therefore, when Jesus had taken the wine, he said "It is consummated!" (Jn 19:30).

These words are no longer imbued with the absolute destitution of *Eli, Eli lama sabacthani*, but already breathe victory and portend the mystery of redemption.

The words of *Eli, Eli, lama sabacthani* embody the ultimate mystery of a suffering to which it belongs that Christ loses sight of his mission to redeem the world through the Cross. The feeling that his heavenly Father has forsaken him implies that the passion is no longer seen in its totality as the mission of the Son of Man. These words are, as it were, the inner aspect of the passion. But in the *consummatum est*, "it is finished," the passion is again seen in its objective aspect, in its totality, in its meaning intended by God. *Consummatum est*: We witness the transition of the plenitude of suffering into victory, a moment which includes a secret of Christ's Heart and, simultaneously, the culmination of the event of all events. *Cor Jesu, pax et reconciliatio nostra, miserere nobis*, "Heart of Jesus, our peace and reconciliation, have mercy on us."

And Jesus cried out with a loud voice and said, *In manus tuas, Domine, commendo spiritum meum,* "Father into thy hands I commend my spirit" (Lk 23:46).

We hear the last words spoken by Christ before his death, the words of which St. Luke says, "And having said this he expired." Here again it is not revelation but the event of the death of our Lord that alone is the theme. It is the supreme donation of his human existence to his heavenly Father, the ultimate expression of absolute surrender, shelteredness, and divine peace. These words are in a certain way the most intimate ones, because they express the very gesture of Christ's rendering his soul to God the Father in a closed I-Thou dialogue with him. But this sublime self-donation to God is also the last effusion of the Sacred Heart foretelling his coming glory.

If the word of the Virgin, "Behold the handmaid of the Lord; be it done to me according to thy word," is the primordial word for our earthly existence, the word of Jesus, "Father into thy hands I commend my spirit," is the final word of mankind, the conclusive word in which the *statu viae* finds its end. It is the pattern of the gesture which man should accomplish in this supreme moment. And yet it is not addressed to us by Christ; rather we are witnesses to this mystery of his heart in the words which the Son of Man speaks to his heavenly Father. It reflects the tension in the mystery of the Incarnation: the Word, the second Person of the Blessed Trinity, the Lord and Redeemer, utters as the Son of Man, the word which is the very summation of man's earthly existence. *Cor Jesu, spes in te morientium, miserere nobis,* "Heart of Jesus, hope of all who die in thee, have mercy on us."

In the appearances of the risen Lord, we find a new stage of the epiphany of God. Not only does the resurrection as such manifest the divinity of Christ, and not only is this mystery the very crown and climax of the epiphany, but in the risen Christ the revelation of the divine quality of Jesus reaches another stage, his divinity is even more transparent. Every word spoken by the risen Christ conveys this divinity in a new epiphany.

The unveiling of his Sacred Heart continues after the resurrection. In the apparition to Mary Magdalene, a glance is granted to us into the Sacred Heart of the gloriously risen Christ. He reveals himself to Mary Magdalene with the one word, "Maria." The very uttering of her name includes in this situation an unveiling of his Heart. A tender love and a glorious joy are present in this making himself known as Jesus. Ineffable intimacy and glory of this situation! On the one hand, the longing of Mary Magdalene, her despair over the Lord's death, her loving desire to find at least his body; and on the other hand, the response of Jesus in revealing himself to her even before the apostles. In disclosing his identity as the risen Christ by the sound of his voice, and by calling her by her name, Jesus unveiled his Sacred Heart.

In the mysterious words, "Do not touch me," the completely new form of existence of the resurrected Christ is revealed. The same Mary Magdalene who had been allowed to wash his feet with her tears and to kiss them was not allowed to touch the risen Lord. And again in the words, *Ascendo ad patrem meum et ad patrem vestrum*, "I ascend to my Father and yours," the holy joy dwelling in his heart is disclosed. *Cor Jesu, vita et resurrectio nostra, miserere nobis*, "Heart of Jesus, our life and resurrection, have mercy on us."

Simon Petrus, diligis me plus quam isti? "Simon son of John, dost thou love me more than these do?" These words, repeated three times by the risen Lord, are spoken by the God-Man Christ, the Redeemer, the one who will come again "to judge the living and the dead."

The appeal to the love of Peter reveals the unfathomable mystery that Christ seeks our love, that he wants not only to be obeyed but also to be loved. It reveals this sublime tenderness, a revelation which acquires a specific import through the fact that it is repeated three times and is one of the last words of Christ. It is related at the end of St. John's Gospel; it is only after all the apparitions of the risen Lord. If the words *mihi est data omnis potestas in coelo et in terra*, "all power in heaven and on earth has been given to me," spoken immediately before the Ascension, are the ultimate revelation of Christ's divinity, the manifestation of his absolute Lordship, these words are the last effusion of his Sacred Heart. They breathe an ineffable meekness and gloriously tender love. And in the divine *Pasce oves meas*, "Feed my sheep," we discern the trembling love for all those who have followed him, for all those who will ever follow him.

Diligis me, pasce oves meae, "Dost thou love me; feed my sheep." In these words, we are offered, as it were, an ultimate revelation of the personality of Christ. And in this total revelation of his Sacred Humanity, the Sacred Heart is the center: *Cor Jesu, deliciae sanctorum omnium, miserere nobis*, "Heart of Jesus, delight of all the saints, have mercy on us."

Part Three
THE HUMAN HEART TRANSFORMED

CHAPTER ONE
The Heart of the True Christian

We have been introduced gradually into the mystery of the Sacred Heart of Jesus, and have tried to grasp both its divine quality and its mirroring of the mystery of the Incarnation.

Against the true glory of the Sacred Heart, "in which shine forth all treasures of knowledge and wisdom," the grave distortion of many hymns becomes obvious. Both in word and in melody these songs not only completely miss the divine, transfigured quality of the Sacred Heart "in which dwells all the fullness of divinity," but they even present the Sacred Heart in the likeness of a mediocre, sentimental human heart. This distortion has evoked an understandable opposition in many people, but an opposition which goes too far in identifying the distortion with the devotion of the Sacred Heart as such. Instead of recognizing the true nature of the Sacred Heart, as presented in its admirable Litany or in the holy Mass of the Feast, one believes that the very fact of a devotion to the Sacred Heart inevitably results in these distortions.

To refute this opposition which confuses distortion with authentic devotion, we have attempted to throw into relief the divine quality of the Sacred Heart by contemplating certain passages of the Gospel. It is necessary to grasp the Sacred Heart in its true glory if the nature and depth of the devotion and its classical liturgical character are to be realized, and if we are to unmask the distortion and ungenuineness in many popular conceptions of this devotion which find their expression in certain hymns and art forms, and even some prayers.

But our attempt to understand the Sacred Heart has another and more positive importance than the correction of distortions. To increase our knowledge of the Sacred Heart, to awaken to a more intimate understanding of it, is a high value in itself. To see the Sacred

Heart in its ineffable glory, and to adore it, is as such of the greatest importance.

This is also indispensable for understanding all the implications of the prayer, *fac cor nostrum secundum cor tuum*, "Make our hearts like unto thine." If we are to understand the transformation in Christ to which our hearts are called, our eyes must see the Sacred Heart of Jesus in its transfigured quality, as the epiphany of God.

The transformation of our ethos depends upon our having a true image of Christ and of his Sacred Heart. As long as we project our own mediocrity and pettiness into the Sacred Heart and nourish ourselves with this image, we remain imprisoned in that mediocrity, instead of being transformed and elevated beyond ourselves. Here as in many other instances we are faced with the great danger of adapting the revelation to our narrow outlook, and of distorting it to such an extent that the challenge to be transformed is lost. Instead of grasping the true face of Christ and the challenge of being transformed, instead of letting ourselves be drawn upward by the love of the authentic God-Man, we miss the confrontation with the epiphany of God.

The question here is not one of disobedience or of rebellion against God. It is a question rather of the quality of the ethos in a man, and the danger that the quality of this ethos will remain untouched by Christ, for then, even with good intentions, one will never attain the transfigured ethos which the saints embody and reflect.

Only now, therefore, having contemplated the Sacred Heart itself, can we hint briefly at the nature of the transformation of our own hearts.

We must however stress from the very beginning the real meaning of this petition prayer. The *secundum* (according to) means that our heart should be filled with the holy affectivity at which we hinted when we quoted words, parables and deeds of Christ. It should be filled with the holy ethos which we find in all saints, the victorious charity, the meekness, the mercifulness, the humility which Christ embodies. But this imitation of Christ never refers to a similarity with the heart of the God-Man from which he lifted the veil, as we tried to show. The unique mystery of the Sacred Heart which implies the fact that this heart is *substantialiter unitum verbo Dei*, "substantially united to the Word of God," is something which cannot be repeated in any saint and which is indissolubly linked to the Incarnation.

To the prayer *Fac cor nostrum secundum cor tuum* applies all that we

find with respect to the meaning of the imitation of Christ. The transformation into Christ which this imitation implies refers to becoming a
saint, attaining a full blossoming of the divine life we receive in baptism when we became members of the mystical body of Christ.

Sometimes, one can hear or read, "act in every situation in the
same way as Christ would have acted." But this is a wrong formulation
of the imitation of Christ. For the God-Man Jesus who said, *Mihi est
data omnis potestas in coelo et in terra*, "All power in heaven and on earth
is given to me," has acted and would act in many situations in a way
which for us to imitate would be a blasphemous exaltation of ourselves,
in the sense given to the word exaltation in the Gospel. The imitation
of Christ should rather be expressed in the words "Act in a way which
can stand the test in a confrontation with Christ, which is pleasing to
Christ, which is in full harmony with Christ," or in the words "act
always in the spirit of Christ." *The similitudo Dei*, "likeness to God,"
which is man's *finis primarius ultimus*, "primary ultimate end," is
synonymous with the *sanctificatio*, "sanctification," of which St. Paul
says, *Haec est voluntas Dei*, "This is the will of God." But the *similitudo
Dei* in no way alters our creaturehood, in no way does away with the
infinite difference between man and God.

We are here concerned with the fruits of grace in the new creature
and not with the mystery of participation in Christ which is constituted by the fact of having received sanctifying grace. We are not concerned with the mystery expressed in the words, "I am the vine; you
are the branches." But what we stated above with respect to our sanctification also applies with regard to this mystery. We are the branches,
but we never can become the vine.

Similarly, we must understand the meaning of the transformation
of our hearts according to the Sacred Heart. It means that we attain the
holy affectivity dwelling in the Heart of Jesus, the true Christian ethos.
But it does not refer to the unique mystery of the Sacred Heart which
is not to be severed from the Incarnation.

Here we must again repeat that the heart has a function other than
the will, and that God has entrusted the heart to "speak" an irreplaceable word, a word which sometimes differs from that to which the will
is called. It would be a disastrous error to overlook this fact and to think
that the heart and will must always speak the same word. To deny that
God has entrusted the heart to speak a word of its own leads to the conviction that the silencing of the heart is a religious ideal.

The call of God directed to our will has to be obeyed, whatever our heart may feel, or however it may object. But this does not at all imply that our heart should conform itself to the will in the sense that it should speak the same word as the will speaks.

Abraham, after hearing God's command that he sacrifice his son Isaac, had to say "yes" with his will. But his heart had to bleed and respond with the greatest sorrow. His obedience to the commandment would not have been more perfect had his heart responded with joy. On the contrary, it would have been a monstrous attitude. According to the will of God, the sacrifice of his son called for a response of Abraham's heart, namely, that of deepest sorrow. But notwithstanding the deep reluctance of his heart, Abraham was obliged to accept this terrible cross and to conform his will to God's commandment.

The God-willed disparity between heart and will which we find in certain cases must not be interpreted as supporting the Kantian notion that a tension between will and heart increases the moral value of the will. In all cases of conflict between the two categories of motivation termed by us the merely subjectively satisfying and value, it is morally preferable that not only the will but also the heart respond with a positive value-response. It is incomparably preferable from a moral point of view if, for example, we rejoice when helping another person, than if we do it only with our will—*à contre coeur*, "against the prompting of the heart." It is far better if our heart flows over with love for our neighbor, than if we only do him good with an indifferent heart.

But our present concern is not with those cases in which a typical morally relevant value challenges us. We are rather thinking of special cases in which a good endowed with high values has to be sacrificed. If we ask, for instance, what the attitude pleasing to God is when a beloved person dies, our answer is that with our free spiritual center we should speak our *fiat*; we should accept the terrible cross imposed on us. This acceptation is an act of will. But it is meant as a cross by God and this implies that our heart bleeds. The cross would have no place in our life if our heart conformed to God's will in the sense that everything that God permits could only gladden our heart. The great and deep mission of the cross would be frustrated if holiness implied that as soon as something sad happens, and thus is at least permitted by God, the heart should no longer worry about it. And not only the role of the cross, but the fully personal character of man, would be frustrated. Man is not simply an instrument, he is a person to whom God addresses himself, whom God treats as a person, since it depends upon man's free will, his free decision, whether or not he will attain his eternal welfare. God also wants man to have his own individual life, to take positions with his heart, to direct himself to God with petition prayers for legitimate high goods in his life. *Deus vult exorari*, "God wants to be asked." And we also pray, *Panem nostrum quotidianum da nobis hodie*, "Give us this day our daily bread."

The Church does not pray exclusively for man's eternal welfare. The possession of authentic earthly goods is included as well as being spared great evils: *A fame, peste et bello, libera nos Domine*, "From famine, plague and war, deliver us, O Lord." Man would be a mere mask, he would no longer have his specific individual life; none of the gifts of God entrusted to him during his life would really reach him; he would no longer have a real history, he would not possess a unique unrepeatable existence, if his heart did not give responses to all real goods—responses of gratitude, of longing, of hope, of love.

Man could no longer live a full human life if his heart spoke the same *fiat* that his will speaks in all those cases where the endangering of a good endowed with a high value, or the loss of it, calls for a specific response of our heart. We emphasize here the sameness of the *fiat*, because the heart also speaks a certain fiat as opposed to any murmuring. The heart also submits to God's will in throwing itself into the loving arms of God, but it does not for that reason cease to suffer. We need only think of the words of our Lord in Gethsemane, *Pater mi, si possibile est, transeat a me calix iste*, "Father, if it is possible, remove this chalice from me."

After having emphasized the specific mission of the heart, we must realize that the transformation of our heart in no way implies a banning of affectivity, which would amount to a silencing of the heart. On the contrary, transformation in Christ implies that the heart is incomparably more sensitive, more ardent, and endowed now with an unheard-of affectivity. At the same time it is purified of all illegitimate affectivity, from any affective response which is not motivated by a value or a high objective good for the person. Moreover it is endowed with a transfigured affectivity, that is, an affectivity which is not only morally legitimate, but one that is sealed with the spirit of Christ, possessing a completely new sublimity, and simultaneously an incomparably greater and deeper ardor.

This point cannot be emphasized too much because certain stoic and oriental influences manifest themselves in certain Catholic currents, old and new. They carry the belief that the imitation of Christ implies that our heart be silenced and only reason and will subsist.

Three stages must be distinguished in this oriental and sometimes even stoic trend. In the first and most radical form, one wants to ban all affectivity and replace it by reason and will. This trend emphasizes knowledge and volition, and gives no place to the heart at all. Effusions of the heart are seen as something inferior to the ideal, something on a low level of perfection which has to be overcome.

In the second form, one admits a role for the heart, but the ideal here is that our affective responses, and especially love, be directed exclusively toward God. No creature should be the object of our love or joy. A certain tendency in this direction is to be found in the early writings of St. Augustine—theses which he later modified greatly—in which he claims that no created good should ever be the object of *frui* (enjoying), but only of an *uti* (using).

The third form allows the affectivity of the new creature in Christ to extend to the love of neighbor. Not only are affective responses to God allowed in the man whose heart has been transformed by Christ, but also love of neighbor and the compassion, joy, and hope which follow from it. Yet even here the affectivity toward creatures remains restricted to the love of neighbor. It is regarded as more perfect if our heart knows no affective responses besides the love of neighbor. To have a specific love for a child, for a mother, for a sister, for a brother, for a friend, or for a spouse is considered as something which, though not illegitimate, is yet less perfect than to know no other affections toward creatures than the love of neighbor. Certainly, they will not deny that all the duties connected with respective relations should be accomplished. But the specific love itself, the full affective response, the delight we take in the beloved, all these are seen as more or less incompatible with a full and complete surrender to Christ.

CHAPTER TWO
Amare in Deo

The Stoic trends we have just discussed are clearly harmful to genuine affectivity. As against these, we should like to stress that no specific love, whether parental or filial, whether of friend or of spouse, is incompatible with the full and complete surrender to Christ, provided only that these loves are incorporated in our love of Christ, and that they are permeated by the spirit of Christ. This transformation in Christ in no way deprives these different loves of their full affective character. Furthermore, it is an error to claim that it would be more perfect, and a sign of a more complete imitation of Christ, if one should know no love other than the love of God and the love of neighbor. As we saw before, our Lord himself loved Lazarus, Martha, and Mary, with a love that cannot be interpreted as love of neighbor. So, too, John the Evangelist who is mentioned as the disciple whom the Lord loved.

Someone could object. The following words also are to be found in the Gospel: *Si quis venit ad me, et non odit patrem suum, et matrem, et uxorem, et filios, et fratres, et sorores, adhuc autem et animam suam, non potest meus esse discipulus*, "If anyone comes to me and does not hate his father and mother, and wife and children, and brothers and sisters, yes, and even his own life, he cannot be my disciple" (Lk 14:26). Do these words not imply that the bonds of natural love are a hindrance for the full imitation of Christ? Are we not entitled to infer from these words that it is more perfect if someone knows no other love than the love of God and of neighbor?

But in reality these words of our Lord in no way justify such a conclusion. They point to the absolute primacy of the love of God, a primacy which demands our readiness to sacrifice a great objective good, such as the enjoyment embodied in personal relations, if God imposes such a sacrifice on us. These words are a reminder that no bond of

human love should ever be a hindrance to our unconditional surrender
to Christ, but they do not thereby deny the goodness, validity, and
compatibility of human love with the love for God. St. Augustine
points to this fact, *Non dico ut non diligas uxorem; sed plus dilige Christum*,
"I am not saying that you should not love your wife, but that you
should love Christ more" (*Sermo* 349, VII, 7, c. 1532 P.L.).

This primacy of love for God applies not only to our relations to
other persons, but as such to any creative work, scientific or artistic or
poetic. These activities should never become the primary and ultimate
theme of man's life. The Rule of St. Benedict which says, ". . . let them
prefer nothing whatever to Christ . . ." (Chapter 72), acknowledges the
need for a readiness to give up anything whenever God demands this
of us. But certainly no one would claim that attachment to artistic, scientific, or philosophical work is of itself a hindrance to our being transformed in Christ, to our full belonging to Christ. Would St. Thomas or
Blessed Fra Angelico have been more perfect had they abstained from
their philosophical or artistic work?

Again, when we read that we should "hate" creatures, we must
realize that these words must never be understood as a commandment
to hate mother, father, or wife. On the contrary, the entire Gospel is
pervaded by the commandment to hate no one. It is clear that the word
"hate" means here simply the readiness to break any human bond if it
hinders us from following Christ, and much more when the alternative
is between following Christ or refusing to follow him because of some
human bond.

The first step in the transformation of the heart is overcoming all
hardheartedness. Every bit of hardness, whatever its source, must be
dissolved under the spell of the Sacred Heart. Our heart's indifference
toward all true values, toward the welfare of our neighbor, toward
offenses against God, or the glorification of God, this indifference
which is the tragedy of so many lives, this bluntness and insipidity of
heart, must be dispelled under the impact of the infinite love of Christ.
Hodie si vocem ejus audieritis, nolite obdurare corda vestra, "Today, if you
hear his voice, harden not your hearts."

The second step is the purification of the heart from all the corruptions that enslave and enfeeble it. We must strive for the liberation of
our heart from the claws of pride and concupiscence. Through Jesus
and in Jesus we should overcome all egocentricity and what we have
called "the tyranny of the heart."

The transformation of our heart must however go beyond a purification from all evil elements. In several prayers of the liturgical year, we hear the words "that we may learn to despise earthly things and to love those of heaven," *terrena despicere et caelestia desiderare*. This prayer clearly refers not only to the right direction of our will, but also to the responses of our heart. In order to understand the transformation of the heart for which the Church prays here, it is necessary to clarify the goods to which the term *terrena* (earthly) refers.

In another book, we analyzed the specific meaning of *terrena*:

Obviously the term terrena (earthly) does not refer to evil and sinful things. Earthly is not the antithesis to morally good. "Earthly things" refer rather to things which are not sinful in themselves, but which are opposed as "earthly" to "heavenly things." It would, however, be just as wrong to identify "earthly" with natural. The fact that the prayer suggests that we should despise "earthly" things indicates that we must still distinguish between earthly and natural goods.

There are many natural goods which we should never despise, such as beauty in nature or art, truth in philosophy and science, and above all friendship and marriage. It is thus of the utmost importance to clarify the meaning of "earthly" in this context.

From the very beginning we must exclude any illegitimate good, or anything which is subjectively satisfying only because of its appeal to our pride or concupiscence. But among legitimate objective goods for the person, we must distinguish between those which are objective goods for us because of their value and those which are good merely because of their agreeableness. To the first type of objective goods belong beauty in art and nature, truth in philosophy, or friendship, marriage, any artistic gift, and any noble talent granted to us; whereas good food, wealth, an influential position, fame, honors—all these delight us, not because of their value, but because they are agreeable to us.

All the goods which are bearers of values reflect God, the Infinite Goodness, Beauty, and Holiness, in their value. They are natural goods, certainly, but they are not "worldly" goods. Granted that every created good can be abused, that we can approach any created good in such a way that it becomes a danger for us, there is still an essential difference between those goods which have as such a kind of "worldly" character, and those natural goods which in no way have this character, but which rather point to a "world above," and a reality beyond this world. These tell us something of God and of heaven. Though earthly in the sense that in their present form they are relative to our earthly existence, these goods nonetheless are resplendent with a value carrying a message from above. If we rightly understand their meaning, they draw us into the depth of our soul and increase our thirst for heavenly goods.

If we emphasize this distinction between worldly goods and earthly ones among natural goods, we certainly do not wish to minimize the difference between the most noble earthly goods and the heavenly ones. One cannot stress enough the completely new and unique character of the supernatural world, of the quality of holiness with respect to the highest natural values. This difference is emphasized when St. Paul says, *Quae sursum sunt quaerite, non quae sunt in terra,* "seek the things that are above, not the things that are upon the earth." Nevertheless, the distinction between "worldly" and "earthly" among natural goods is of fundamental importance for the Christian life. The attitude of the true Christian to the "worldly" and to the non-worldly natural goods, which are however earthly and not heavenly, should be a different one. The Christian should not seek worldly goods, and when they are bestowed upon him, without his having striven for them, he should *use* them, remaining aware of the danger which they include, aware that as soon as we start enjoying them for their own sake, they are prone to thwart our full concentration on Christ. Because in the very quality of these goods there is an antithesis to the supernatural world, their "worldly" character makes it impossible to yearn for them without some alienation from Christ.

Natural goods endowed with a high value, on the contrary, call for another response. Their value, when rightly understood, has the character of a message of God, a reflection of his infinite beauty. Thus, an enjoyment of them for their own sake, our praying for them, need not be incompatible with the full desire for heavenly goods (*Not as the World Giveth,* pp. 70–72).

Thus it seems that within the framework of natural goods an important distinction has to be made, so that the despising of the *terrena* is understood as referring only to the "worldly" natural goods and not to those natural goods endowed with a high value.

Moreover, one must understand the great difference between desire for a good and grateful appreciation of it when it is bestowed on us by God. The desire to be wealthy, for example, is from a religious point of view very different from the grateful appreciation of wealth which is bestowed on us through an inheritance, or as a gift, or through some such source. The grateful appreciation implies, however, that we are not completely indifferent to the good in question. Of course, it may be that we have a specific vocation for poverty, in which case we must give away to the poor the money bestowed on us. But if no such vocation exists, then the many goods endowed with an authentic value, for whose enjoyment wealth is a means, justify our grateful joy at receiving the gift. Between this grateful joy and the desire for wealth, however, there is evidently a wide chasm. But the *despicere terrena* requires more than the mere absence of desire for goods like wealth. It requires first that wealth not be considered as a good in itself. Needless to say, there are many who take the opposite view and consider wealth as such a good. The social position granted by it, the security and freedom from worries, the *Lebensgefühl* (worldly well-being) bestowed on us by wealth, are indeed all elements which make wealth a good as such, if we avoid all illegitimate satisfactions like the feeling and exercise of power. Wealth as such, then, can be very attractive, but the transformation of our heart requires that it no longer be attractive to us. We may however consider wealth as a gift because it is a means to many goods endowed with a high value, for it grants us the possibility of helping our neighbor, of bestowing gifts on those we love, or of supporting projects of genuine value; and it makes possible many goods for ourselves, such as visiting beautiful countries, possessing an artistically beautiful home, and so forth.

But even this attitude of looking at wealth as a means to higher values is not enough. The transformation of our heart by Christ requires above all that, in receiving such "worldly" goods as wealth, we acknowledge the full responsibility their possession implies, that precisely the above-mentioned *Lebensgefühl* of the wealthy, the security and the social position, must be replaced by a trembling heart. The feeling of master should give way to the attitude of servant. This also applies to other worldly goods, such as a high office or fame.

From all such "worldly" goods, then, our heart must keep an inner distance; it must possess them in the spirit of St. Paul, "As having nothing, yet possessing things."

Concerning those goods which, though natural goods, have no "worldly" character—the goods which are endowed with values and thus bear a qualitative message from above—another attitude is required in the transformation of our heart. There can be here no question of *despicere*. It is rather the *amare in Deo*, "the loving all things in God," which here marks the transformation of our heart. This attitude implies not only that we love Christ above all, but also that our love of all other things is incorporated in Christ. Thus, for example, beauty in nature and art should be enjoyed in Christ. This does not mean that we should consider the beauty in question only as a starting point for meditation about Christ. It means rather that this fully appreciated beauty draws us in *conspectu Dei*, that we find in its own quality a ray of God's infinite beauty, and that we hear in it the voice of Christ. The same applies to the knowledge of natural truth. We should seek it *in Deo* and enjoy its possession *in Deo*.

The attitude demanded in these two cases also differs from the attitude toward worldly goods insofar as the longing and seeking for these goods here in no way contradicts the transformation of our heart by Christ. Certainly this longing and seeking must be incorporated into our over-all relation to God; it must be subordinated to the primary desire for *caelestia*, ("heavenly goods"), i.e for our sanctification and eternal union with God. The *ordo amoris*, "the order dictated by love," requires that the desire, the longing, and the seeking be in conformity with the objective hierarchy of goods. Yet, not only is this desire legitimate, but our praying to attain the enjoyment of these goods is in no way contrary with the full surrender to Christ.

The desire for such noble goods, however, should always be embedded in the abandonment to God's will. Furthermore it is essential that when we long for the enjoyment of these goods, they be approached as reflections of God's infinite beauty; they should elevate us above the "worldly" goods and draw us toward God. There is, after all, an indirect revelation of God in the created world, as the words of the Liturgy testify, "The heavens and the earth are filled with thy glory." Those created goods endowed with sublime value should not be considered as a mere occasion of mortification; they have a positive mission for man. But they should never be idolized, and they should never be separated from God, never detached from the inner link they have with God; their message from God should never be ignored.

Something analogous to this should mark our attitude toward the highest of all earthly or created goods, namely, our communion of love with other persons, such as the relation between parent and child or between friends, and above all, between husband and wife. Here again there can be no question of despising such high and noble goods. The Christian attitude willed by God is here too the *amare in Deo*—*amare* being taken here in the most literal sense of the term.

In the first part of this book we analysed the high value of affective value-responses, and of the "being enraptured" by a high and noble affectivity. We also saw the danger inherent in man's fallen nature of tumbling down from intense affective value-responses into a turmoil of passion. Now we must emphasize that only in Christ and through Christ can this danger be overcome. It is precisely one of the characteristic results of the transformation of our heart by Christ that we are able to experience the true "being enraptured" by something greater than ourselves while being protected from falling out of the *religio*, "the bond with God." Only when our entire affective life is rooted in Christ and penetrated by the love of Christ, only when our heart is wounded in a loving adoration of his most Sacred Heart can the state of "being enraptured" by a creature be liberated from the danger of gliding from "holy madness" into the passionate state of "being out of our mind." We said above that affectivity as such can never be too intense, too strong. We must add now: this is true in Christ, true for the man whose heart has been transformed by Christ. It is to this man that the words of St. Augustine find their full application, *dilige, et fac quod vis,* "love, and do what you will."

Transformation in Christ endows us with a new freedom. The one who accepts the yoke of Christ, which is sweet, will also be liberated insofar as he need no longer fear that the plenitude of affectivity may lead him to the danger of going astray. The one who has become a *captivus Christi,* a slave of the love of Christ, attains the freedom of no longer being hampered and hindered in the flow of a sanctioned love for a creature. He is freed from the fear of letting himself be enraptured, from the need of moderating the blissful plenitude of his love.

This should not, however, be understood in the sense that through one act of abandonment to Christ, we come into a state in which we could simply follow the immanent logic of a love for a creature. No, union with Christ must be constantly renewed. Yet our remaining in the *religio* is not guaranteed by a reserve attempting to channel our love from without by building dams with our reason, which all lead to a frustration of "being enraptured" by the love for a creature. On the contrary, the confrontation with Christ which is ever in need of being renewed and in which our hearts are permeated again and again by his spirit, by the rays of his Sacred Heart, grants us the bliss of "being enraptured" without falling out of the *religio*.

We have hinted at the nature of the transformation of our heart through Christ and the contemplation of his Sacred Heart.

But in this book, the mystery of the Sacred Heart as such was our main theme. Thus we wish to conclude it by repeating again what we stressed in the introduction, namely that the adoration of the Sacred Heart cannot be severed from the adoration of the Sacred Humanity of Christ.

Let us realize how life, nay the entire world, becomes more meaningful, more beautiful, more glorious when another aspect of Christ's Sacred Humanity—always implicitly contained in revelation—is made explicit by the Church. Explicitness is a great gift.

In the Sacred Heart we are confronted with the very core of the Sacred Humanity of Christ and by that, with the very secret of the mystery of the Incarnation, of the union of divine and human nature in the God-Man.

Contemplating the Sacred Heart of Jesus, gratitude, never-ending gratitude fills our hearts, and we cannot but join the voice of the Church in the preface of the Feast of the Sacred Heart:

> It is indeed fitting and right, our duty and our salvation, that we should praise and glorify you at all times, Lord, holy Father, almighty and eternal God, for you decreed that your only-begotten Son should be pierced by a soldier's spear as he hung on the cross, so that a stream of grace and forgiveness might pour on us from his riven heart, the treasure-house of divine bounty; and that this heart, never ceasing to burn with love for us, might be the place of rest for those who are faithful and the safe refuge of those who repent. (Translation used in the *Layman's Daily Missal*.)

Appendix: Introduction to the 1965/77 Edition of *The Heart*

By Dietrich von Hildebrand

Inspired by our Lord in a vision, Sister Droste-Vishering asked Pope Leo XIII to offer the entire world to the Sacred Heart of Jesus. Her request was received with that reserve which the Church maintains in the face of private revelations. Sister Droste-Vishering continued to pray and to sacrifice for her great mission. For three years she was bedridden, suffering terribly. After much deliberation by highly competent theologians, the Holy Father finally decided to yield to her request. On the very day that the bells of all Catholic churches rang out proclaiming the solemn act of consecration of the world to the Sacred Heart of Jesus, Sister Droste-Vishering died. She had accomplished her great and sacred mission.

Every year the Church relives the history of man's redemption in its liturgy. In this display of its sacred, intimate life, we find an alternating rhythm. Each liturgical season stresses a different event in the history of man's redemption; and thereby, in each season, another aspect of the mystery of the Incarnation and of our redemption is thrown into relief. This alternating rhythm of the liturgy is dictated by the fact that the liturgy commemorates and reenacts man's redemption as it has unfolded in time. But the alternating stress on the different aspects of one and the same divine reality is also imposed by the very nature of man *in statu viae*. It is not possible for man in this earthly life to comprehend at once and fully the entire body of revealed truth, or to give a full response to all its manifold aspects. This will be possible only in eternity.

The necessity of approaching the different aspects of one and the same mystery alternatingly is demonstrated also by the variety of extra-liturgical devotions. Many of these stress one or another aspect of the mystery of the Incarnation, for example, the devotion to the divine

Infant Jesus introduced by St. Francis of Assisi, or the devotion to the passion of our Lord, or the devotion to the Sacred Heart. Each one is directed to Christ, the God-Man, in the light of a single aspect which throws the mystery of the Incarnation into fresh relief. Thus, the figure of a child eloquently expresses humanness in its limitation: man born of woman as a helpless babe, and submitted to a development starting from this helpless condition, reaching progressively the status of an adult. Hence in the divine infancy, the tension between the absoluteness of God and the limitedness of the finite creature gloriously shines forth. And in the Infant Jesus, God's infinite charity, manifesting itself in the taking on of flesh, is revealed in an exquisitely touching manner.

Again, in the adoration of Christ in his passion, this tension between the divine person and the divine nature, on the one hand, and Christ's human nature, on the other, discloses itself overwhelmingly. It is the eternal God, the Second Person of the Holy Trinity, the Word, who suffers in his human nature. And the reality of this human nature is impressively revealed, for to be subject to suffering is a specific mark of a human person. And just as it was in the devotion to the Infant, the mystery of God's infinite charity is adored in this devotion. True, the mystery of charity is already contained in the Incarnation itself, but the passion of Christ manifests in an overwhelming way the infinite love of Christ for us.

But it is perhaps in the adoration of the Sacred Heart that the mystery of the Incarnation and of God's infinite charity manifests itself in the deepest manner. In the invocation, *Cor Jesu, in quo habitat omnis plenitudo divinitatis*, "Heart of Jesus, wherein abides the fullness of the Godhead," we find the tension that is immanent in the mystery of the Incarnation in its full, ineffable glory. In saying *Cor Jesu*, we are touching on the deepest and noblest mark of human nature, to have a heart capable of love, a heart which can know anxiety and sorrow, which can be afflicted and moved, is the most specific characteristic of the human person. The heart is the most tender, the most inner, the most secret center in man, and it is in the heart of Jesus that the plenitude of Divinity dwells.

And what an extraordinary emphasis on the infinite love of Christ in the Sacred Heart, on this mystery which is the deepest source of our joy! That Christ loves us is the great secret, the most intimate secret of every soul. It is the most inconceivable reality; it is a reality which would completely change the life of every man if he could but realize it fully. This realization requires not merely a theoretical knowledge of this mystery as a revealed truth, but an awareness of this love similar to one's awareness of the love of one's beloved. And it also implies an awareness of the incomparable character, the unique character of this divine love, its absolutely new and mysterious quality, its ineffable holiness, such as shines forth in the Gospel and the Liturgy, and is mirrored in the lives of the saints.

This great secret—God's infinite love for us in Christ—which is the source of our joy, our consolation, our hope *in statu viae* and our everlasting joy in eternity, shines forth in a specific way in the Sacred Heart: *Cor Jesu, fornax ardens caritatis*, "Heart of Jesus, glowing furnace of charity."

It is a principle governing the life of the Church that in the course of time the one revealed truth is more and more differentiated. The development in the field of dogma (very often elicited by heresies) clearly testifies to this process of an ever more explicit formulation and emphasis.

Thus in its infallible magisterium the Church not only protects the eternal, unchanging, supernatural truth, but also offers through this differentiation an antidote to the specific errors of a given time. Just as in the Gospel our Lord stresses different aspects of the all-embracing truth according to the person to whom he is speaking and the specific danger to which he is pointing, so the Church makes different aspects of the one unchangeable truth more explicit while counteracting the specific dangers of an epoch.

Something analogous is also found in the development of different devotions. Here too we witness this process of differentiation, that is, that a devotion whose object was always implied in a revealed truth is in the course of time thrown into greater prominence. This differentiation is a process of growth having its meaning and value in itself. It may be elicited by the errors of an epoch or, providentially, it may anticipate these errors. A new devotion may thus have a double relation to the errors of an epoch: it may be an antidote to present errors, or it may be providential armor put on against coming dangers.

Devotion to the Sacred Heart has, primarily, the character of an inner differentiation, the explicit unfolding of something always implied in the adoration of the Sacred Humanity of Christ. But it is also a providential response to the aberrations of an epoch and the heresies of an ethos. In the seventeenth century when this devotion

was introduced, it was, apart from its intrinsic meaning, both an antidote against Jansenism and a providential armor for the future. In the
increasing emphasis on it in our own time, we find the antidote to such
errors as anti-personalism and "neutralism" of the heart. At a time
when hatred is directed against human personality, when a radical fight
is being waged against the dignity of man, and when an impersonal
indifferentism threatens the world, the Sacred Heart radiates the light
of the infinite divine love: *Et lux in tenebris lucet,* "and the light shines
in darkness." The unarmed Heart of Jesus, exposed to all injuries and
offenses, all blasphemies and attacks, unknown to an innumerable
multitude, misunderstood and ignored in its divine message by many
others, reveals always anew that the ultimate reality is love: *Deus cari-
tas est,* "God is love."

It has been said at times that our religion should be theocentric
rather than Christocentric. It is argued that since Christ himself was
constantly directed to the eternal Father, we should follow his example. And it is argued further that he is the Mediator and that the
Church prays: *per Christum Dominum nostrum,* "Through Christ our
Lord." But as we already said in another work, these are alternatives
that do not apply to the supernatural realm.

> In reality, it is a mistake to oppose these two forms of rela-
> tionship with Christ. Christ is both the eternal Word of the
> Father addressed to us, God's epiphany, and the mediator
> between us and God, our Head through whom alone we may
> adequately adore God. Christ eternally turns his face both
> toward the Father *and* toward us. He is not only one who leads
> us to God like Moses; he not only stands at the side of human-
> ity looking up at God together with humanity and leading it to
> God, but he also stands before us, as the self-revelation of God,
> as he who speaks to Philip, "Philip, he that seeth me, seeth the
> Father also," and of whom St. John says, *Et vidimus gloriam
> ejus, gloriam quasi unigeniti a Patre, plenum gratiae et veritatis,*
> "And we saw his glory, the glory as of the only-begotten of the
> Father, full of grace and truth."
>
> Our bond of union with Christ is not only a "we-commun-
> ion," in which the exclusive Thou is God the Father; our bond
> of union with Christ is also an "I-thou communion." In the giv-
> ing of ourselves by love to Christ, in becoming one with him,
> we are drawn into the most holy Trinity.

Though our "we-communion" with Christ, our membership in his Mystical Body is ontologically constituted in supernatural fashion through baptism, it would, nevertheless, remain dead without the giving of ourselves through faith and love to Christ. Thus, especially the full transformation into Christ will never be achieved in us without the "I-thou" communion with Christ.

Once again we find in the Liturgy both these aspects in their mysterious interpenetration. In the holy Mass, we sacrifice with Christ, our Head; he is turned toward the Father, and he does not turn away from the Father when in holy Communion his face is turned toward us, and through this communion of love with him, we are received through his holy humanity into his Godhood" (*Liturgy and Personality* pp. 126–27).

Thus we may say: the more Christocentric, the more theocentric.

The center of Christian revelation is the self-revelation of God in Christ. The crowning of all Christian revelation is the epiphany of God in the Sacred Humanity of Christ. As the preface for Christmas expresses it: ". . . for the light of your glory has flooded the eyes of our mind anew in the mystery of the Word made flesh, and through him whom we recognize as God made visible may we be caught up into a love of things unseen."

But still one hears the objection: Why must the heart be the object of a special devotion? Is not what has been said for the devotion to the Sacred Heart contained in the adoration of Christ, the God-Man, in his Sacred Humanity? What does this relatively new devotion add?

We have already mentioned that any emphasis on one aspect of the mystery of the Incarnation, far from drawing us away from the entire personality of Christ, helps us to immerse ourselves in that personality, that is, to contemplate him in a more awakened way and to adore him more intimately. It is, however, revealing that the objection raised against the devotion to the Sacred Heart is not raised against the devotion to the Infant Jesus, nor to the devotion to the passion of our Lord. The very objection implies a failure to understand the specific aspect of the divine mystery which devotion to the Sacred Heart discloses.

In other works we have stressed as one main mark of Christian morality the totally new and central role granted to charity. Whereas rectitude and justice are the core of natural morality, in Christian

morality the specific center is the goodness of charity. It is this luminous goodness with its breath of mercy which envelops us when we
hear the parable of the prodigal son. "But while he was yet a long way
off, his father saw him and was moved with compassion, and ran and
fell upon his neck and kissed him" (Lk 15:20–21). It is this same goodness of superabundant charity whose impact we again feel in reading
the parable of the Good Samaritan. It is this quality which plays so
incomparable a role in Christian morality.

In this luminous and victorious goodness, the voice of the heart
plays a predominant role. If we compare the glorious martyrdom of St.
Stephen as told in the Acts of the Apostles with the noble death of
Socrates as described in Plato's *Phaedo*, we cannot but grasp the completely new role played by the heart in the followers of Christ. In the
martyrdom of St. Stephen, there is a noble spirituality that involves the
superabundance of the heart.

Indeed, a transfigured affectivity permeates Christian morality. It
is an affectivity that differs fundamentally from any natural affectivity.
But this difference does not consist in less ardor, less tenderness, less
affectivity. On the contrary, it is a limitless affectivity, one which discloses new and unheard-of dimensions of the heart. "I have come to
cast fire upon the earth, and what will I but that it be kindled?"
(Lk 12:49).

Devotion to the Sacred Heart throws into relief the mystery of this
holy affectivity of the Sacred Humanity of Christ, and does so with all
the realism so characteristic of Christ's revelation.

By this realism we mean the individual, concrete character of
God's revelation in Christ as opposed to any abstractionism that confuses authentic breadth with logical extension; it is opposed as well to
any proud spiritualism which scorns matter. The breadth of individual
concrete reality pervades the entire Gospel as well as the Liturgy. We
find it again in St. Francis of Assisi and in the Franciscan movement.
It is also found in a specific way in the adoration of the Sacred Heart.
Here, a concrete realism manifests itself in the way in which the
Sacred Body of Christ is drawn into the devotion. The fact that the
devotion is extended to this bodily heart which has been pierced by
the spear of the soldier, from which his Sacred Blood dripped, gives to
the entire devotion an implacable realism. The mysterious interpenetration of the physical heart and the heart as spiritual center of affectivity immerses us in the concrete reality of this blissful mystery. We

are confronted with the same ineffable quality that also touches us in the veneration of the Sacred Blood, the same mysterious sobriety, so abysmally deep and ineffably sublime. *Quis est iste, qui venit de Edom, tinctis vestibus de Bosra?* "Who is this that cometh from Edom with dyed garments from Bosra?"

We mentioned before that the Church makes explicit in a given moment what was always present implicitly. The Sacred Humanity of Christ continually radiates the message of his Sacred Heart in his unfathomable divine love. Although the devotion to the Sacred Heart was introduced relatively late and has increased more and more in our own time, it is nonetheless true that the mystery of the Sacred Heart shines forth through all the centuries since the advent of our Lord. The Apostles were under the spell of the Sacred Heart. The words, "For I am meek and humble of heart," moved the souls of all his followers. We hear in the Liturgy the words: *Improperium exspectavit cor meum et miseriam: et sustinui, qui simul mecum contristaretur, et non fuit: consolantem me quaesivi, et non inveni: et dederunt in escam meam fel, et in siti mea potaverunt me aceto,* "My heart hath expected reproach and misery; and I looked for one that would grieve together with me, and there was none: I sought for one to comfort me, and I found none; and they gave me gall for my food, and in my thirst they gave me vinegar to drink." *Popule meus, quid feci tibi; aut in quo contristavi te? Responde mihi,* "O my people, what have I done unto thee? or in what have I offended thee? Answer me." Here we are confronted with the Sacred Heart of the Lord.

Throughout the Christian era, the Sacred Heart has always been "the delight of all saints," *deliciae sanctorum omnium*. Devotion to the Sacred Heart only renders explicit a reality which was always present in the sacred life of the Church. Far from seeing devotion to the Sacred Heart as a special modern cult alien to the spirit of the Liturgy, we should understand that it organically grows out of the adoration of the Sacred Humanity of Christ.

In the face of this most intimate and tender mystery, all deviations of a merely natural human affectivity, such as mediocrity and egocentrism, are unmasked. A confrontation with the Sacred Heart, *fons vitae et sanctitatis*, "source of life and holiness," also unmasks the shallowness of all affective neutralism, all false "sobriety," and all idols of non-affective reasonability, hypertrophy of the will, and of a pseudo-objectivity. The Sacred Heart of Jesus, *Cor Jesu, de cujus plenitudine omnes nos accepimus*, "of whose fullness we have all received," dispels all attempts to reduce love to obedience, the plenitude of the heart to reason and will, as well as all attempts to eliminate the most personal ardor, the true "subjectivity," from the Christian ethos.

But in order to delve deeper into the mystery of the Sacred Heart and to see its glory in its proper light, in order to grasp the specific aspect of the Incarnation which shines forth in the Sacred Heart, we must first discover what the true nature of the heart is. If we are to understand the transformation to which our hearts are called, if we are to seize the full impact of the prayer, *Fac cor nostrum secundum cor tuum*, "make our hearts like to thine," we must first discover the meaning and the role of the heart in man. In short, we cannot understand the devotion to the Sacred Heart in its true meaning, or in its specific mission to melt our hearts, unless we first discover the true nature of the heart, and the grandeur and glory of true affectivity.

The role that the Church grants to the devotion to the Sacred Heart, and the increasing emphasis laid on this aspect of the mystery of the Incarnation, carries with it a great challenge—namely, that we deepen our understanding of the heart as one of the fundamental centers in man's soul. What we divine in contemplating the Sacred Heart—the glory of the mystery of the Sacred Heart of Jesus which emanates and flashes forth from the Litany of the Sacred Heart; its invocations, the length and breadth and height and depth of the love of Christ which penetrates the Liturgy of the Sacred Heart—all this calls imperatively for an exploration of the nature of "heart."

The prayers at the foot of the altar at the beginning of Mass reveal the mystery of man's heart to us. They lead us up the heights and down the abysses of the human heart. A changing rhythm of holy joy, "metaphysical" anxiety, loneliness, trust in God, hope envelops us. We hear the words, *Ad Deum qui laetificat juventutem meam*, "To God Who giveth joy to my youth," and then suddenly the *quare tristis incedo*, "why do I go sorrowful," again the *qui laetificat juventutem meam*, "Who giveth joy to my youth," and after the *quare tristis es, anima mea*, the *Spera in Deo*, "Hope in God," and then again *qui laetificat juventutem meam*.

We realize the central role of the heart in all its depth and, at the same time, are made aware of the mystery of its alternately changing rhythm in man. The entire Psalter offers the same aspect of the centrality of the heart. And anyone who has ears to hear cannot but be aware of the great and glorious voice of the heart in the Prophets and the words of our Lord.

But when we read anything philosophical dealing with the heart and the affective sphere, we find a completely different picture. This center of man is presented as less serious, less deep, and less important than his intellect or will. Here we are confronted with a drastic example of the danger of abstractionism, that is, the danger of constructing theories about reality without consulting reality. This is a philosophical approach which must inevitably fail to do justice to reality. The role of the heart in man's life, in the Liturgy, and in the Holy Scriptures, on the one hand, and the heart and the affective sphere in the world of philosophical theory, on the other: two different worlds!

As a matter of fact, the heart has not been given a real place in philosophy. Whereas the intellect and the will have been made the object of searching analysis, the phenomenon of the heart has been largely neglected. And whenever it has been analyzed, the heart has never been given a standing comparable to that of the intellect and the will, a standing that would do justice to the genuine importance and rank of this center of the human soul. Invariably the intellect and the will have been placed much higher than the heart.

Should not the fact that it is precisely the heart of Jesus which is the object of a specific devotion, and not his intellect or will, move us toward a deeper understanding of the nature of the heart, and consequently to a revision of the position taken toward the entire affective sphere?

Yet such an investigation is of great importance even apart from this challenge to explore the nature of something which has been chosen by the Church and by divine providence to be the object of a specific devotion; and it is important apart from the fact that a knowledge of the nature of the heart is indispensable for a better understanding of the great mystery which the Litany of the Sacred Heart expresses in the words: *Cor Jesu, in quo habitat omnis plenitudo divinitatis*, "Heart of Jesus, wherein abides the fullness of the Godhead."

Devotion to the Sacred Heart is exposed to distortions and misinterpretations more than any other devotion. As Cardinal Newman said, every popular religion is in some way corrupted; and his words can be especially applied to the sublime devotion to the Sacred Heart. Many devotional pictures of the Sacred Heart and especially many hymns, in their words and their melodies, display a mawkish sentimentality, and portray the Sacred Heart not only stripped of supernatural mystery but, even from the natural point of view, as insipid and mediocre. Unfortunately, in order to counteract this danger, one offers against this "soft" conception of the heart, a conception which portrays the heart in a kind of merely natural strength which, moreover, is tainted by pseudo-virility. To insist, then, that the Sacred Heart must be regarded, not as soft and effeminate, but in its "virile" strength is merely to move from Scylla to Charybdis. A cheap virile pathos is as mediocre as a sugary sentimentality. Both are distortions and falsifications of the true nature of the heart even in the purely natural frame. And, needless to say, such aberrations falsify our conception of the Sacred Heart itself.

Clearly then, such misconceptions call for an elaboration of the true nature of the heart.

It is, patently, not our aim to offer a doctrinal treatise on the theology of the Sacred Heart; there are competent theologians who are equal to this task. The magnificent encyclical *Haurietis aquas*, of Pope Pius XII, of glorious memory, offers the theological basis of this devotion from the highest authoritative source. In this book rather we shall endeavor first, to expound the nature of the heart in an attempt to do full justice to the depth and spiritual plenitude of this center of man's soul, and thereby to pave the way for a deeper penetration into the ineffable mystery of the Sacred Heart; for only when we understand the role the heart plays in man can we see that in the Sacred Heart of Jesus we are confronted with a specifically deep and significant aspect of the Incarnation.

In the second part of this work, we shall try to shed light on some aspects of the mystery of the Sacred Heart so that our eyes may be opened to the inexhaustible riches and glorious beauty of this mystery.

A final part will be devoted to the transformation to which our heart is called. Not only should our intellect be enlightened by Christ, not only should our will be directed to God in Christ and through Christ, but also our hearts, which have an irreplaceable mission in human life, should be transformed in Christ. As the prayer says: *Fac cor nostrum secundum cor tuum*, "Make our hearts like to thine."

May God's infinite bounty grant us that our efforts may increase our understanding of Jesus Christ, and love for Him, through the contemplation and adoration of his Sacred Heart, *in quo habitat omnis plenitudo divinitatis*, "in whom dwelleth the fullness of the divinity."

Dietrich von Hildebrand
1889–1977

Dietrich von Hildebrand was an original philosopher, religious writer, heroic anti-Nazi activist, courageous Christian witness, and passionate proponent of beauty and culture. Born in 1889 as the son of a famous German sculptor, von Hildebrand grew up in the rich artistic setting of Florence and Munich. He studied philosophy under Edmund Husserl, the founder of phenomenology and a giant of twentieth century philosophy, and under Adolf Reinach, and was profoundly influenced by his close friend, German philosopher Max Scheler, who helped to pave the way for his conversion to Catholicism in 1914.

By 1930 von Hildebrand had become an important voice in German Catholicism, perhaps best known for his pioneering work on man and woman and on marriage. One can trace the chapter on marriage in *Gaudium et spes* of Vatican II back to von Hildebrand's writings in the 20's in which he argued that the marital act has not only a procreative meaning but a no less significant unitive meaning. But he also distinguished himself in other ways during his years at the University of Munich, most of all through his ethical writings and through his book, *The Metaphysics of Community*, in which he used the resources of phenomenology to rethink fundamental issues of social philosophy and of moral philosophy. Von Hildebrand had a profound affinity for beauty, which he never considered a mere luxury but a human necessity. In his last years, this lifelong passion came to fruition in his magisterial two-volume study in the philosophy of beauty, the *Aesthetics*.

When Hitler came to power in 1933, von Hildebrand left his native Germany, and dedicated himself to resisting Nazism. He moved to Vienna and founded a journal for combating at the level of philosophical first principles the rising Nazi ideology and for defending the independence of Austria against Germany. With the German occupation of Austria in 1938, von Hildebrand became a political fugitive; fleeing through Czechoslovakia, Hungary, Italy, Switzerland, France, Portugal, and Brazil, he eventually arrived in the United States in 1940.

Von Hildebrand wrote many works unfolding the faith and morals of Catholicism, such as *In Defense of Purity*, *Marriage*, *Liturgy and Personality*, and, above all, *Transformation in Christ*, now recognized as a classic of Christian spirituality.

In the United States von Hildebrand taught at Fordham University until his retirement in 1959. Many of his most important philosophical works—among them *Ethics*, *What is Philosophy?*, *The Nature of Love*, *Morality and Situation Ethics*, *The Heart*, and *Aesthetics*—were completed in the United States.

Through his many writings, von Hildebrand contributed to the development of a rich Christian personalism, which in many ways converges with that of Karol Wojtyla/Pope John Paul II.

Von Hildebrand died in New Rochelle, New York, in 1977.

Index